RULES OF THE LENDING GAME

HOW TO MASTER THE GAME OF LENDING TO INVEST IN PROPERTY

STUART WEMYSS

First published in 2020 by Major Street Publishing Pty Ltd
E | info@majorstreet.com.au
W | majorstreet.com.au
M | +61 421 707 983

Quantity sales. Special discounts are available on quantity purchases by corporations, associations and others. For details, contact Lesley Williams using the details above.

Individual sales. Major Street publications are available through most bookstores and can also be ordered directly from Major Street at www.majorstreet.com.au.

Orders for university textbook or course adoption use. For orders of this nature, please contact Lesley Williams using the details above.

The moral rights of the author have been asserted.

A catalogue record for this book is available from the National Library of Australia

ISBN: 978 0 6486626 5 5

Cover design by Simone Geary
Internal design by Production Works
Printed in Australia by Ovato, an Accredited ISO AS/NZS 14001:2004 Environmental Management System Printer.

10 9 8 7 6 5 4 3 2 1

Disclaimer: The material in this publication is in the nature of general comment only, and neither purports nor intends to be advice. Readers should not act on the basis of any matter in this publication without considering (and if appropriate taking) professional advice with due regard to their own particular circumstances. The author and publisher expressly disclaim all and any liability to any person, whether a purchaser of this publication or not, in respect of anything and the consequences of anything done or omitted to be done by any such person in reliance, whether whole or partial, upon the whole or any part of the contents of this publication.

CONTENTS

ABOUT THE AUTHOR

Stuart Wemyss is a licensed independent financial adviser, registered tax agent, chartered accountant and licensed mortgage broker. He has over 20 years of financial advisory experience and founded his Melbourne-based practice (ProSolution Private Clients) in 2002.

Stuart's goal is to inspire people to take action to achieve their lifestyle and financial goals through advocating the benefits of holistic and independent advice. Many important financial decisions involve numerous financial disciplines such as taxation, financial planning, risk management and borrowing; he therefore believes people will maximise their wealth if they receive holistic and honest advice.

Stuart writes a weekly blog which he also records as a podcast called *Investopoly*. He regularly contributes articles to the Wealth section of national newspaper *The Australian*.

He is married and has two teenage sons, whose only advice to him is 'Dad, put the pen down'. Suffice to say that his sons aren't avid readers of his books (yet)! Stuart's passions include travelling to new destinations with his wife, all things French, red wine, enthusiastically supporting the Geelong Football Club and spending time with his family.

You can follow Stuart's musings on LinkedIn (linkedin.com/in/stuartwemyss) and Twitter (twitter.com/StuartWemyss).

ACKNOWLEDGEMENTS

I would like to thank my beautiful wife for her unwavering love and support. She does so much to support me at work and at home: everything from bringing me coffees while I wrote this book to helping me navigate important life and business decisions. She looks after me so amazingly that everything I achieve personally (such as writing this book) is the result of her contribution. I couldn't do it without you. I love you very much.

My personal goal is to inspire people to achieve their lifestyle and financial goals through advocating the benefits of holistic and independent (honest) advice. It's why I write books like this one, record podcasts, publish blogs and choose to do the work I do. The team at ProSolution Private Clients has been helping me work towards this goal now for nearly 18 years. Thank you to all the staff for your dedication to doing work that you're proud of. I'd especially like to thank the two longest-serving members, Jodi McKeown and Kristy Dishon, who've been working with me for well over a decade. Thank you, ladies.

WHY YOU NEED THIS BOOK

When I applied for a mortgage to buy my first property at the age of 24 (many, many years ago!), I had no idea what I was doing... with the mortgage and with life in general! There were so many mortgage options and so much different terminology that I couldn't make head or tail of it, even though I was an accountant at the time.

I was more excited about buying a property and building wealth than about the boring mortgage. I just wanted to know that the bank would give (lend) me the money and that was pretty much it. The mortgage was a mere distraction.

I ended up putting my trust in a mobile banker from one of the 'Big Four' banks (the Big Four are the Commonwealth Bank, ANZ, NAB and Westpac, and we'll discuss these further throughout the book). The mobile lender came out to see me at home. I didn't speak to anyone else for comparison purposes, and there were no online mortgage comparison websites or access to the enormous volume of information that is available online today. I didn't spend much time considering cash flow and affordability. I didn't think about my future needs or the future use of the property. I probably didn't even ask about the interest rate! I pretty much just said, 'Show me the money' and went on my merry way.

I think my experience would be similar to that of a lot of people. A mortgage is a means to an end; it's really nothing to get excited about... or is it? Well, I'm going to propose that it is something to get excited about. I believe that building wealth and getting ahead financially is a game of finance. And those who know how to play the game get ahead. Most people consider mortgages to be liabilities. However, if used correctly (and I'm going to show you how), a mortgage can be an asset – a very powerful and effective asset.

The rules have changed

Prior to 2016, getting a mortgage approved was easy-peasy! You would just walk into a bank and tell them what you earned, and they would typically be prepared to lend you way more than you would ever feel comfortable borrowing. You'd hardly have to provide any documentation, sometimes you wouldn't even have to sign an application form, and the lender certainly would not ask you what you spent your money on and how much cash you had left over. Lending policies and processes were very loose – definitely too loose.

That all changed after 2016 – and dramatically so. The process of applying for a mortgage these days is like a criminal forensic financial investigation. It's intrusive. It's laborious, and often pedantic. But you can make it easier by becoming 'borrowing ready'. I'll tell you how.

Why read a whole book about mortgages?

If you find it hard to get motivated to ensure you're structuring your loans correctly, then imagine how hard it is to write a whole book on the subject! I completely understand that people generally fall in love with the idea of buying property, not with taking out a mortgage. I get it.

Think about it this way, though: every person in the world has a borrowing limit. There's only so much money a lender will be prepared to lend you, so it's a scarce asset. Therefore, you must think very carefully about how you use that scarce asset. Use it wisely and it's more likely that you'll achieve your financial and lifestyle goals.

The three main things that determine your personal borrowing capacity are:

1. cash flow
2. equity
3. risk tolerance and financial stability.

The way you go about structuring your mortgage can dramatically affect your maximum borrowing capacity. A poorly structured loan portfolio will choke cash flow, waste equity and expose you to higher risk. This means you borrow less... and guess what? For those property-lovers but mortgage-haters out there, it means you buy less property, invest less and/or don't reduce non-tax-deductible debt at the fastest possible rate. This probably means you create less wealth and you're further away from financial freedom.

So, my advice to you, if you're turned off by the topic of mortgages, is to read this book once and once only. Then, immediately go out and find yourself a trusted credit adviser. This book will give you knowledge to select the right adviser – someone who's an expert, not an amateur or just a good salesperson. Once you have the best adviser you can find, hang onto them throughout your investment journey. This approach will allow you to focus on the sexier side of the undertaking – investing in the property, shares and the like – and means you'll be able to maximise and optimise your borrowings throughout your life.

What you don't know will hurt you

Boy, do I have a surprise for you. I guess you've probably heard the saying, 'You don't know what you don't know until you know it'? Well, it couldn't be more apt when it comes to structuring loans. I founded my financial advisory business in 2002. Prior to this, I was working at one of the international accounting firms, Deloitte, but a moment of insanity led me to think that building a successful business would be an enjoyable challenge. I resigned from Deloitte and literally two weeks later I was sitting in my apartment feeling pretty confident about starting a mortgage-broking business because 'How complex can mortgages really be?' Remember, by that time, I already had a mortgage, which had been nice and simple to arrange and hadn't taken up much of my time.

What I learned (very quickly) was that a mortgage can in fact be easy. However, it's as easy to establish an incorrect loan structure as it is to establish a perfect loan structure – that's the problem. You often don't realise you have the wrong structure in place until afterward – sometimes many years later. Frustratingly, you may have to live with your mistakes, because often they can be too costly or difficult to correct. Therein lies the problem. Mortgage structuring can be insidious, and it's deceptively easy to make a mistake.

It's not often that I meet a new client who hasn't made a costly mistake with a mortgage in the past. Many people make the same mistakes. They go it alone, thinking it's a simple process, and learn through error that in fact they should have paid more attention to their financing. That's generally when they come to see me. Frankly, it makes my job a lot easier, because they immediately value my advice. Other people's mistakes have also provided me with heaps of ideas for the many articles I have written over the years, which have resulted in this book.

Get it right but keep it simple

I don't want to make things any more complex than they need to be. I like simplicity: it's easier to understand, easier to manage and typically lower cost. Often, it's possible to keep things simple and yet still get things right.

This book will teach you everything you need to know about borrowing that I've learned over the past 17-plus years. I've tried to take what can be complex concepts and make them as simple as possible, and have endeavoured to ensure that the information in the book is communicated in a way that allows you to implement the ideas which are relevant to you straight away, so you get immediate value from my strategies.

I cover basic topics such as:

- the best products to use and when to use them
- how to manage your cash flow effectively and maximise your borrowing capacity
- how to maximise current and future borrowing tax deductions, and
- how to develop a good financial strategy so that you can safely and effectively build wealth.

I then delve a little deeper and give you a step-by-step description of how and why you should structure loans in a certain way. Importantly, due to my background (being a chartered accountant, tax agent and financial adviser) – and because tax and lending are heavily interrelated – I cover the tax considerations. My aim is that, by the time you've finished reading this book, you'll know more about mortgages than your average mortgage broker or lender.

In chapter 14, I've provided a summary of the key takeaways from each chapter. This will help you avoid making mistakes when you're in the throes of arranging and reorganising your loans, as it serves as a quick and easy reminder.

A WORD ABOUT JARGON

All industries have their own language and the mortgage industry is no different. Don't be put off by the jargon: 'borrowing', 'gearing' and 'leverage', for example, are one and the same thing – using other people's money. For your convenience, I've included a glossary at the back of the book.

It's not just about property

Although the majority of mortgages are used to fund property investments, the principles explained throughout this book can be applied to all forms of borrowing – for example to purchase a business or to invest in shares or managed funds or real estate investment trusts.

This book is guaranteed to save you money – every year!

Interest is the single largest lifetime expense for an investor. The amount of debt investors carry affects their net worth and their cash flow, and can make or break their retirement goals. I guarantee that getting your borrowing right will save you a considerable amount of money in the short term and over the years. It's not uncommon, in fact, for the advice I give my clients on structuring their investments to save them well over $10,000 per year.

This is not a sales pitch for my business; it's a sales pitch for this book. Never underestimate the value of the right structural advice! It's a gift that keeps on giving, as good advice results in recurring savings. On the other side, beware: a poor structure will continue to cost you money each and every year. The cost of this book, plus the few hours of your life you'll invest in reading it, is a very small price to pay compared to what you'll gain from it.

Good luck! I'd love to receive your feedback. You can connect with me in a few ways:

- I have a weekly blog which is also a podcast – www.prosolution.com.au/blog
- I frequent Twitter – @StuartWemyss
- I spend a bit of time on LinkedIn, too – www.linkedin.com/in/stuartwemyss

Most importantly, if you like this book, please share it. Tell your friends and family, and if you're willing to do so, post a review or recommendation of it somewhere online. The more people that read it, the more people will, hopefully, benefit.

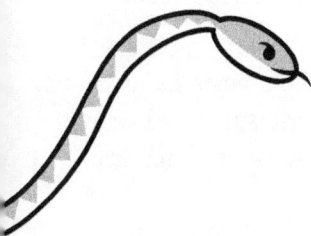

1.

THE PLAYERS

Smart borrowers have an understanding of all the lenders in the marketplace, and of their individual pros and cons and when to use each one. I call them the 'players'. You need to know the players in any game; how else can you back the winning team? New players come in and out of the market, so it's useful to have an understanding of where the game is currently at in an historical context. A quick history lesson will give you a deeper insight into the workings of the mortgage market and, in turn, greater confidence when approaching lenders.

A history lesson

The finance industry has changed dramatically over the past 25 years. Once upon a time, hopeful home buyers had to dress up in their 'Sunday best' and approach their local bank manager in an attempt to secure a loan.

Prior to 1980, the finance industry was heavily regulated. This prevented smaller players from getting a foot in the door and offering alternative products to those offered by the major banks, who held a definitive market monopoly. In the early '80s, however, the federal government realised that competition in the banking industry was desperately needed in order to expand the options available to consumers and keep the 'Great Australian Dream' of home ownership attainable.

So, a decade of systematic deregulation of the finance industry began in 1981, breaking down some of the barriers that had kept the power players in control for so long. Although this marked the beginning of a somewhat easier ride for new lenders, it was still slow going due to the regulatory red tape involved in getting a banking licence.

However, as the 1990s and early 2000s progressed, more and more lenders entered the marketplace, all vying for borrowers' business and offering hundreds of loan products with far less stringent approval criteria than previous generations of borrowers had had to meet.

Perhaps the most significant change during this deregulatory phase – and the biggest thing to hit the finance industry – occurred in 1992, when Aussie Home Loans was launched by John Symond, AM. Anyone born in the 1970s or earlier will probably remember Aussie's 'We'll save you' TV commercials. Before 'Aussie John' broke into the finance arena, the banks were making a profit margin of more than 4 per cent! Aussie John saw this profiteering, recognised the opportunity it presented and approached Adelaide Bank for wholesale money – to become a lender himself through a process called 'securitisation', which we'll discuss later in the book. He was able to make some serious waves by undercutting the banks' margin by about 2 per cent; this bold move encouraged other smaller competitors to enter the market and brought the bigger banks into line.

It changed the market forever. Credit unions, smaller mortgage managers and other wholesale lenders such as RAMS (who are now owned by Westpac) progressively opened their doors to more and more home buyers seeking finance, once they could see a more level playing field.

Now, the major banks' profit margins (called 'net interest margins') are around 2 per cent, according to the Reserve Bank of Australia, and even lower for some of the smaller lenders trying to keep up in an increasingly cut-throat area. Essentially, Aussie John was the catalyst that forced the banks to halve the margin they'd been enjoying for so many years. Although we all gripe about current bank fees, if you add up the total revenue made from mortgages 20 years ago – including fees and the net interest rate margin – and compared it to what we pay today, in percentage terms consumers are now much better off.

That was really what the federal government hoped to achieve when it decided to deregulate. Deregulation opened up the banking industry and made it a lot more competitive, which benefited the consumer and encouraged more people into the housing market. Previously, there was really nothing driving or incentivising the banks to offer better deals to customers. They were naturally more concerned about their shareholders and the bottom line.

The global financial crisis in 2008

The global financial crisis (GFC) has largely been blamed on the bad lending practices of banks worldwide – particularly in the US and Europe. When the credit-crunch came (i.e. when it came time to pay back these loans), defaults on a monumental scale caused banks to go under.

In Australia, due to our stricter regulation and tougher lending criteria, our banking industry held firm. The government played a part in this by underwriting the banks during this difficult time, which meant that customers were guaranteed that their deposit funds would be safe, come what may. The government also lent its AAA rating to the banks to help them access funds from overseas.

These measures were criticised by many, because the fee charged for the lending guarantee was too high for the smaller lenders and so damaged competition, feeding the Big Four's dominance.

During the GFC, many smaller and second-tier players were acquired by the Big Four, giving them even more power in the marketplace. The government just sat on the sidelines and didn't object. Aussie Home Loans, Wizard and Bankwest were bought by the Commonwealth Bank of Australia, and Westpac purchased St. George and RAMS. Suncorp nearly went bust but managed to remain on its feet, mainly because no-one wanted to buy it and it had to find its own solutions.

Essentially, there aren't many lenders now, post-GFC, that are independent of the Big Four. This has given the Big Four even more market power and reduced competition, in my view.

Credit tightening from 2017

The banks' regulator, the Australian Prudential Regulatory Authority (APRA), started talking about tightening credit policy in late 2016. In early 2017, it released an updated regulatory guide (APG 223) which, among other things, required banks to make more enquiries into a borrower's living expenses. The banks made some significant and severe changes to their own policies as a result. The upshot is that, when you apply for a loan, banks will typically trawl through the most recent three months of your bank statements in order to determine how much you spend. They don't distinguish between discretionary and non-discretionary expenditure; as I said earlier, it's tantamount to a forensic investigation.

In March 2017, APRA became concerned about the volume of interest-only mortgages – that is, mortgages for which the repayments comprised only interest, and the borrower was not obligated to repay any of the loan's principal. At the time, over 40 per cent of all new mortgages were interest-only. APRA's response was to demand that the banks reduce new interest-only loans to less than 30 per cent; when the banks well and truly achieved this target by late 2018, APRA removed the benchmark.

The consequence of these two changes (living-expense checks and reduced interest-only lending) is that the loan-application process has become significantly more difficult, onerous and time-consuming than it has been in the past.

The Royal Commission in 2019

The Royal Commission into Misconduct in the Banking, Super-annuation and Financial Services Industry was established in December 2017 and conducted its hearings throughout 2018. It handed its final report to the Governor-General on 1 February 2019.

The Royal Commission didn't make any recommendations that would materially impact the mortgage market, other than recommending that mortgage-broker commissions be banned. The government has shelved that recommendation, as it recognised that it would be a disaster for the mortgage-broking industry and probably result in its demise – ultimately handing more market power to the big banks. The banks pay mortgage brokers a commission, which I view as a 'tax' that the banks must pay due to the otherwise low level of competition in the marketplace. In other words, mortgage brokers facilitate increased competition between banks, so the banks must pay for their existence to ensure that there's a good level of competition.

It's all about the margin

The banks might incessantly grumble about the low margins they make from home-loan lending, but it's unlikely they'll ever enjoy the levels these rates were at prior to deregulation. In fact, I think there may even be further margin contraction. In the UK and US, lenders are making less than 1 per cent on their home loan rates; although they're very different markets, I believe that we'll see further erosion of the banks' margins here in Australia. However, the US and UK finance industries are more fragmented than ours – their largest banks don't hold anywhere near the 80 per cent market share enjoyed by the Australian Big Four.

Of course, a loss of revenue due to margin contraction has meant the banks have tried to counteract that dip in profits – primarily by focusing on bank fees. Consumers have reacted angrily to more and more fees and charges being introduced; however, they perhaps don't realise that they're still better off paying these costs than returning to the days when the banks had larger margins.

So, while the Australian market has made some progress, I think something dramatic has to happen before there's another large shift in terms of competition. I just can't see it happening any-time soon.

The Big Four

So, who's competing for your business today? Most of you will be familiar with the Big Four players: National Australia Bank (NAB), ANZ (Australia and New Zealand Banking Group Limited), Commonwealth Bank of Australia (CBA) and Westpac Banking Corporation. As I noted earlier, the Big Four's market share increased greatly during the GFC – peaking at over 90 per cent after their acquisition of many of the smaller lenders. Today, some smaller lenders have been successful at winning customers back, and the Big Four's market share hovers around 80 per cent (according to KPMG).

St. George, BankSA, Bank of Melbourne, Bankwest, Wizard and Aussie Home Loans are all owned and controlled by the Big Four, despite many of them still operating under their previous branding.

The four big banks are obviously very powerful financial institu-tions with large balance sheets. They offer a full range of products to clients, meaning that if a borrower establishes a relationship with one of the big banks (as opposed to a smaller lender), they can cover off all their product needs – financial advice, property loans, share broking, the works.

A bank is a place that will lend you money if you can prove that you don't need it. —Bob Hope

Second-tier lenders

What about some of the smaller lenders that have made the industry more affordable for us over the years? Let's take a look at how the finance-industry lightweights stack up against the heavyweights.

The Big Four are well known and recognised brands; however, some second-tier lenders have spent a lot of marketing dollars to get noticed. You're probably familiar with the likes of ING, Suncorp, Bank of Queensland, Members Equity (ME) and Bendigo Bank. They do their best to compete with the Big Four, but there are some differences. For example, sometimes their credit policies are more restrictive and conservative, particularly for investors and people with a lot of lending.

Credit unions and building societies

Credit unions and building societies are generally cooperatives, with many operating as not-for-profit organisations. They are usually formed by the aggregation of their 'members', who typically all work together in a specific industry, business or organisation; for example, Woolworths Employees' Credit Union and Police Credit Union Limited.

Rather than aiming to make profits for shareholders, traditionally, credit unions and building societies offer a service to their members. They take deposits from members and use that deposit base to lend money to customers. (They're now becoming a little more competitive in how they finance their mortgage books, but that's beyond the scope of this book.)

Many credit unions applied for banking licences after the GFC because they wanted to start calling themselves 'banks' (which you can only do if you have a licence), to convey stability to existing and new members. For example, Ford Co-operative Credit Society now trades as Geelong Bank and Victoria Teachers Credit Union now trades as Bank First. They're still owned by their customers.

Working with a customer-owned cooperative that isn't driven to generate profit might sound like an attractive alternative to banking with the Big Four. However, credit unions and building societies have problems keeping up with the banks in terms of providing the full range of services. They might offer products such as personal loans and home loans, but they don't generally offer services such as financial planning, share trading or funds management, which is a potential disadvantage.

Also, these institutions don't have the scale that the big banks do, so their costs are typically higher. They might not make a profit, but that doesn't always mean they can deliver products at a lower cost.

Mortgage managers

Mortgage managers act as intermediaries, rather than actual product manufacturers or market makers. A mortgage manager will approach a wholesale funder such as Advantedge (NAB) or the Adelaide Bank (a lot of the larger banks sell wholesale mortgage funds) and ask for a lump sum of money to re-lend to their clients at a higher margin. For example, if I were a mortgage manager, I might approach Adelaide Bank and request a wholesale facility of, say, $20 million. I would then on-lend these monies to my clients. I might pay Adelaide Bank 3 per cent and charge my clients 4.5 per cent, thereby making a gross profit of 1.5 per cent.

As they're merely intermediaries, mortgage managers are not required to have banking licences. Their funder or funders take care of all the red-tape requirements on their behalf. Larger mortgage managers may have two sources of funding, whereas smaller players might only have a single source. They can have their own delegated lending authority, so they can approve loans on behalf of the bank that funds them, but they still have to comply with that bank's credit policies. In this respect, they almost work like a sub-branch of a larger lender.

During the GFC, many mortgage managers saw their sources of funding dry up or the funding costs spiral out of control, which permanently damaged a lot of these businesses – RAMS, for example, which is now owned and funded by Westpac.

These days, many mortgage managers attempt to create their own brand in the industry by targeting a specific market segment, so they don't have to compete with the banks; for example, offering only small commercial loans, self-managed super fund (SMSF) loans, non-conforming loans or 'low-doc' loans.

Generally speaking, they don't offer any products or services apart from mortgages, and therefore can't take deposits or operate like banks. They might have a branded credit card associated with their wholesaler but, ultimately, if you choose to establish a lending relationship with a mortgage manager, all you'll probably get is a mortgage.

Neobanks and online lenders

Online lenders have been around for more than ten years, with the highest-profile lender being UBank, owned by NAB. Online lenders can be a good solution for borrowers with very simple needs who don't need advice or assistance from a human; however, most of the customers I've spoken with tell me that setting up a mortgage online can be very 'clunky', especially if something doesn't go to plan. That's when you need a human to call upon. So, they won't suit some borrowers, such as first home buyers and investors.

A neobank is a bank that is totally digital: that is, it doesn't have any branches or large call centres. Instead, it uses technology, artificial intelligence and machine learning to interact with its customers via apps and online services. There are currently five neobanks in Australia (being 86 400 Ltd, Volt Bank Limited, Xinja Bank Limited, Archa Pty Ltd and Judo Bank Pty Ltd), all at different stages of evolution, and only one, 86 400 Ltd, offers mortgages so far – although I expect the others to follow soon. It will be interesting to see if they're able to compete with the Big Four, and to what degree.

Non-conforming lenders

Non-conforming lenders, such as Liberty Financial and Pepper Money, target borrowers who don't conform to mainstream credit policies. These may include, for example, borrowers with defaults listed on their credit file, ex-bankrupt persons, and people who have been self-employed for only a short time. In an environment where credit is very tight, more borrowers are being classified as non-conforming.

Of course, non-conforming loans typically attract higher interest rates.

Private lenders or private funds

Private lenders or private funds are something of a dying breed. They generally consist of wealthy private individuals or businesses which have money available to lend out as mortgages. In the past, much of this lending was conducted through solicitors' funds, where the solicitor might have a number of wealthy clients whose money was pooled together and then re-lent to private clients – acting in much the same way as a mortgage manager.

Again, these private lenders generally selected a niche to work within. For instance, in the late 1990s and early 2000s, if you had a bad credit rating due to a default or bankruptcy, the only lenders that might consider providing you finance would be private lenders.

However, the arrival of non-conforming lenders such as Liberty has substantially reduced the very specific pool of people that these solicitors or private funds lend to. These days, the only way private lenders can get any money out there in the market is if they offer short-term lending solutions or 'mezzanine finance' (typically a loan secured by a second mortgage or caveat) to property developers. If people need fast cash for a deposit to purchase a property or something of that nature, a private lender may perhaps loan them $50,000; they charge a very high rate of interest in most cases.

Where do lenders get their money?

When you're considering which type of lender to approach, it's important to have an understanding of how they fund their mortgages, as this could impact on your application being accepted, rejected or subject to the additional cost of lenders mortgage insurance (LMI).

There are three main ways a lender can fund mortgages:

1. through a deposit base
2. via domestic and/or international money markets (through bonds and similar instruments)
3. by securitisation.

We look at all three of these in detail.

PLAYING TO WIN

Astute borrowers know that not all lenders are equal. Dealing with a deposit-base lender, a securitised lender that must insure its loans or a small credit union that has customer limits can be very different. Selecting the wrong type of lender will hamper success.

Deposit base

Deposit-base lenders are quite literally lenders who take deposits, such as banks and, in some cases, credit unions and building societies. Depending on their capital adequacy requirements (that is, the required ratio of equity to deposits and mortgages held at any given time, which is set by government agency APRA), they can take a portion of their money and re-lend it as mortgages.

Keep in mind that there are still many traditionalists out there who have a lot of money tied up in their bank accounts. While this might not earn them a great deal of interest, their loyalty does provide the banks with a very cheap and flexible source of funding. The Commonwealth Bank has the biggest deposit book in Australia, which means that, mathematically, it could also offer the cheapest cost of funds in this country (depending on the make-up of its funding).

Money markets

Money markets have been used by lenders as a source of funding a lot more since the GFC. A bank or lender borrows money from 'the market' – which includes investors and institutions such as superannuation funds and insurance companies – by issuing bonds. The higher rated the lender is (i.e. the safer they are), the more cheaply they can access funds. An AA-rated bank, for example, will be seen as a low-risk borrower (issuer of bonds) and therefore will be able to source more money at a lower rate than smaller, 'more risky' banks. This is where the Big Four have a major advantage over second-tier lenders with lower grade credit ratings, and (after the GFC) lenders that couldn't afford the government lending guarantee fee.

Securitisation

Securitisation isn't a new concept; however, it only came to the fore in the finance industry in the early 1990s. It's essentially a process of pooling a large number of individual mortgages and then reselling them back to the wholesale market. These are typically called 'mortgage-backed securities' (MBSes).

Normally, lenders will aggregate mortgages with similar credit strength. So, they might have $100 million worth of mortgages at an average charge rate of 4 per cent which they will then sell back to the market at perhaps 4.5 per cent or 5 per cent.

Institutional investors such as superannuation funds and large corporations traditionally bought these mortgages, secure in the knowledge that the capital they put in was backed by residential properties. This gave them peace of mind in terms of the creditworthiness of the finance, and they benefited from a higher rate of interest than they might receive on deposit or investing in bonds.

When the GFC began, the securitisation market all but closed overnight, with only a couple of transactions completed over the following 18-month period. This meant that some lenders no longer had access to any funding, nor did they have the ability to roll over old funding. No-one in the world wanted to buy mortgage-backed securities, because no-one knew which mortgages were toxic (i.e. at risk of default or already defaulted on). In 2009, the Australian government started buying MBSes in an effort to get the market moving again, but the securitisation market remains a shadow of its former self.

Everything moves in cycles, so I'm sure securitisation will be back. However, lenders have probably learned not to rely so heavily on a single source of funding, and are aware that property values can drop dramatically, as was seen in the US during the GFC.

The primary benefit of securitisation is that the lender can shift its lending off its balance sheet; for example, mortgage managers can repay their wholesale facility and start again. I mentioned capital adequacy earlier – lenders can only take a certain amount of deposits to disperse for loans, because they must make sure they always have enough money available if people want to make withdrawals from their accounts. Capital adequacy requirements ensure banks maintain a safe amount of liquid assets and equity, keeping them financially strong. Securitisation, however, allows banks to move mortgages off their balance sheet so they can reallocate capital (or need less capital).

One of the potential drawbacks for customers of some of these securitised lenders is that they often require their mortgages to be insured, so that the subsequent mortgage-backed securities receive a lower risk rating. Normally, the bigger lenders who fund their mortgages from their balance sheet will only insure loans with a loan-to-valuation ratio (LVR) of more than 80 per cent. This means that if you want to purchase a property valued at $800,000, for example, you'd need to have a deposit of 20 per cent, or $160,000.

On the other hand, securitised lenders have a policy of insuring all loans, regardless of the LVR. Whether they then on-charge the expense of mortgage insurance to the borrower often depends on the LVR in consideration. Most lenders pay the cost of insuring the mortgage themselves if the borrower is seeking a mortgage below an LVR of 80 per cent, but charge the cost to clients who are borrowing above 80 per cent, in order to stay competitive with balance sheet lenders.

The downside of securitised lenders

The requirement for mortgage insurance on a loan from a securitised lender – under all circumstances and at any LVR – can constrain serviceability or the types of securities that mortgage insurers will accept. For example, if you wanted to buy an apartment with a small living area, even if you intended to borrow less than the 80 per cent threshold, you could be knocked back due to the insurer's policies. You're more likely to get a thumbs-up on your application for the purchase from a Big Four or larger second-tier lender which can fund your loan via means other than securitisation.

There's simply less flexibility in using lenders who purely securitise.

Let's take another example of the more rigid requirements of a securitised lender. In this scenario, you approach the CBA seeking 82 per cent borrowings and ask them to waive lenders mortgage insurance because you have a strong application. They can analyse applications on a case-by-case basis and may agree to your request, potentially saving you thousands in insurance fees. If you approached a lender like Resimac with the same request, by contrast, they wouldn't even consider it. They always have to pay mortgage insurance, and for any borrowings above 80 per cent, they will always on-charge this cost to the customer.

Investors who intend to borrow large amounts, perhaps spread across multiple loans, should give this point further consideration. Most mortgage insurers have an individual borrower exposure limit and will only insure loans up to $1.5 and $2 million per client. If you use a securitised lender, therefore, they might cap your total lending at $2 million, even if your LVR is less than 80 per cent. You need to take this into account for future borrowing ability, too – for example, if you want to increase the loan in future to access equity.

Mortgage insurers: the puppeteers

All of us are aware of the role lenders play when it comes to making or breaking our chances of getting into the real estate game. In fact, one of the first things we think about when buying a home is generally who we'll approach for a loan.

Most people give very little thought to the puppeteers behind the lenders – the lenders mortgage insurers that in many instances pull the strings and make the ultimate decision as to whether or not we obtain a mortgage. More and more borrowers are seeking to borrow more than 80 per cent of a property's value, which will subject them to a mortgage insurer's scrutiny, so it's important to understand what these faceless entities are and how they operate.

Mortgage insurers are third parties to the banks. The two largest mortgage insurers in Australia, QBE and Genworth Financial, effectively form a duopoly, controlling 97 per cent or thereabouts of the market share. In early 2019, APRA approved another mortgage insurer, Arch (listed on the US Nasdaq) to operate in Australia: this may generate some welcome competition.

Mortgage insurers sell their products to lenders, insuring them for any loss should they need to sell the insured security (property) due to loan default by their customers. The larger the percentage of a property's value that an institution is lending to a client, the greater the risk to the lender that they will make a loss if things go wrong and they have to sell the property to recover funds.

Let's look at an example, in which a bank lends a client 95 per cent to buy a home, but shortly after this, the market dips a little and the client can no longer afford to make the loan repayments. The bank might only realise 90 per cent of the property's value, should it take possession of the property and sell it (known as a 'mortgagee sale'). This leaves a shortfall of 5 per cent of the initial borrowings. In this case, the mortgage insurer pays the difference and the bank breaks even.

Recently, mortgage insurers have come under fire, accused of adding to the problem of the ongoing housing affordability crisis in this country, as theirs is just another expense to add to the overall cost of purchasing a property. According to Genworth's *FY19 Financial Results Presentation* of 5 February 2020, only around half of one per cent of mortgage insurers' contracts are ever acted upon – in other words, they're rarely forced to pay up on the loans they insure and are arguably making an enormous amount of money for doing nothing. This is particularly the case in a rising market, because as property values increase, the insurers' exposure is reduced, as lenders are more likely to realise the full amount of any loans they're forced to recoup through mortgagee sales.

Lenders mortgage insurance premiums have increased significantly since the GFC. Both LMI companies in Australia used to be owned by American companies and were thus exposed to the epicentre of the GFC. (Australian company QBE purchased US-owned insurer PMI during the GFC; Genworth is still American-owned.) However, large losses were not experienced in the Australian market, so there was no reason for such large premium increases.

In fact, it's probably only over the first two to three years of a loan that lenders are exposed to any potential loss. Further down the track, more breathing space is created between the value the property will realise on the open market and the loan amount, which is being reduced via repayments.

The issue of mortgage insurance is generating fierce debate within the real estate and finance industries, but I believe only a major catalyst – such as an increase in competition – will stir things up and change the situation. It's long overdue in the eyes of many, and would be most welcome.

Creditors have better memories than debtors.
—Benjamin Franklin

What does lenders mortgage insurance cost?

Mortgage insurance rates are generally charged as a percentage of the loan amount plus stamp duty. The percentage rate depends on two factors: the dollar amount borrowed and the loan-to-valuation ratio (LVR). The table following sets out some indicative rates, to demonstrate how the percentage charged increases with an increase in loan amount and/or LVR. For example, if you purchased a property for $570,000 and borrowed 90 per cent of its value (or $513,000), the mortgage insurance premiums could be 2.50 per cent of this loan amount (or $12,825).

LVR	Loan amount		
	$500,000	$750,000	$1,000,000
85%	1.00–1.20%	1.15–1.40%	1.20–1.40%
90%	2.40–2.80%	2.15–2.70%	2.15–2.60%
95%	2.96–3.40%	4.00–4.70%	4.00–4.70%

The cost of mortgage insurance varies significantly between lenders, so it's something you need to speak with them about directly. Often, borrowers don't even think to ask what the going rate of mortgage insurance is. They focus solely on the interest and fees applicable to a loan, even though the cost of mortgage insurance can vary by thousands of dollars, which is quite significant in the scheme of things.

Note that most lenders cannot vary the cost of mortgage insurance (i.e. it's a non-negotiable cost), as it's normally paid to a third-party. Insurance usually kicks in at an LVR of anything above 80 per cent; however, some lenders will consider lending up to 85 per cent without mortgage insurance, so the lines are somewhat blurred in this regard.

Picking who you'll play the game with

Each type of lender has various pros and cons and, in order to make sure you get the best deal possible, it's important that you weigh up their overall merits. Consider what they can offer you, not simply the rates they charge.

Here's a summary of some of the differences we've discussed in this chapter:

- Balance-sheet, 'deposit-base' lenders can provide more flexibility in loan approvals, as they're the sole decision-makers.

- Larger lenders can offer more bundled banking products to their clients. You may be able to negotiate a free banking and transaction account, for example, a lower rate on your mortgage and/or a free credit card.

- Mortgage managers who work within a niche sector of the market can be of benefit to relevant borrowers in that niche.

- Credit unions can be attractive to people who like to feel as though they're part of a family or dealing with a smaller, more personal business, rather than simply being another faceless number among the big banks' 10 million customers.

It's rare that a one-size-fits-all approach is appropriate. For investors, using a combination of different types of lenders can sometimes yield the best results, as it evens out all their differing pros and cons at a portfolio level.

Mortgage broker or direct to the lender?

The final consideration, when examining the evolution of the finance industry and how it currently works, is the emergence of mortgage brokers in the late 1990s and early 2000s. Mortgage brokers were once a rare commodity and borrowers were forced to sweat out the loan-application process in front of their bank manager, but now, according to the Mortgage & Finance Association of Australia (MFAA), approximately 55 per cent of new loans are taken out via mortgage brokers. This market share continues to grow each year.

Establishing a relationship with a mortgage broker can bring significant benefits. Brokers represent a number of different lenders (often more than 30) and therefore can advise which lender offers the best product for your situation. This can save you a lot of time shopping around. However, you could simply create your own spreadsheet to compare these costs.

I think the real 'value add' is a broker's advice on things like loan structure and credit policy. A good broker will have all the knowledge this book contains, and probably more! For example, if you wanted to purchase a property with a living area of 40 square metres, a mortgage broker should be able to advise you which lenders will lend against that type of security. Also, and perhaps more importantly, if you plan to invest in several properties to create wealth, then a good mortgage broker can develop a longer-term credit strategy to allow you to make your investing goals a reality. Helping you achieve your financial goals sooner is a very valuable service.

As with most things, it's the quality of the person you deal with that will determine the success of the relationship. There are some excellent bankers and brokers in Australia; an excellent banker will probably offer more value than an average broker and vice versa. However, the most fundamental difference between a broker and a lender is that the broker offers choice (i.e. products from a number of different lenders) and isn't employed by or tied to one particular lender. Therefore, they're more likely to tell you the good, the bad and the ugly. They don't necessarily care which lender you use, as long as they win your business.

When was the last time your bank proactively called you up and told you that because their competitors are offering a lower rate, they've decided to match it and reduce your current interest rate? Never, right? And it's probably never going to happen. However, good mortgage brokers do this all the time, because they need to retain your business and want to earn referrals.

Establishing a relationship with a banker (i.e. an employee of a lending institution) can be beneficial too, particularly if you run your own business and have extensive needs. However, even then, I typically advise clients to separate their transactional business banking and their borrowings and have these with two different lenders, so you have full control over access to information.

PLAYING TO WIN

Finance is a game which is ultimately played to help you achieve lifestyle and financial goals. Building a relationship with a good banker or mortgage broker is paramount to winning this game. Professional advice will save and make you a lot more money in the long run than a slightly cheaper interest rate. So, maintain perspective about this. You need a good banker or broker on your team if you're going to be successful.

Make sure your advisers are licensed

In 2011, the government introduced a requirement that all lenders, banks and mortgage brokers – anyone giving credit advice – had to hold an Australian credit licence, under the *National Consumer Credit Protection Act 2009*. The aim was to ensure tighter regulation of the people providing credit advice and to legally require them to ensure that any credit advice they give is appropriate. Perhaps the most significant advancement was the introduction of a requirement for the credit adviser to investigate and document why they feel that the product or products they're recommending are 'not unsuitable' for the borrower – a pretty low burden of proof in my opinion.

One of the recommendations made by the banking Royal Commission in 2019 was to include a 'best interest' duty in the law – a provision that credit advisers must act in the borrower's best interest – which seems like a pretty obvious and basic requirement. At the time of writing, this Bill* was before the Australian Parliament but had not yet been enacted into law.

In any event, if someone offers you mortgage advice, make sure they're licensed to provide it.

---

* The not so succinctly named Financial Sector Reform (Hayne Royal Commission Response – Protecting Consumers (2019 Measures)) Bill 2019.

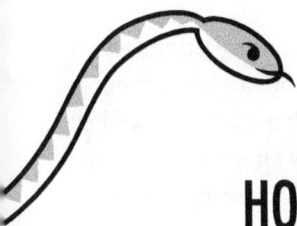

2.

HOW MUCH SHOULD YOU BORROW?

Now that you know more about the lending industry and the major players, let's look at the most frequently asked question by borrowers: 'How much *should* I borrow?' This is a more important question than 'How much *can* I borrow?', which we'll address in the next chapter.

Playing the long game

Why do you want to borrow money? A desire to 'outdo the Joneses' or try and become wealthy overnight can be real driving forces for people getting into the real estate game. That's why there are so many spruikers of get-rich-quick schemes out there, telling us we can make millions from property in a matter of minutes. But this is unrealistic. Playing the long game and making money with careful, considered investing isn't.

The problem is that this often involves getting into enormous debt. That four-letter word, 'debt', and the idea of having to borrow multiple hundreds of thousands of dollars, can really scare some people away from investing. With today's ever-changing lending environment, interest-rate moves and housing affordability challenges, however, more and more punters are at risk of borrowing beyond their capacity.

Now, more than ever, it's essential to know your limitations when it comes to borrowing funds to start or continue to buy property – or to invest in any other asset classes, for that matter. Whether you're seeking a loan to purchase property as an owner-occupier or an investor, or whether you're considering getting a margin loan to buy shares, ask yourself the same question: 'How much is enough?' How do you measure your personal maximum borrowing capacity – how much are you comfortable borrowing? And what happens if you get into trouble and struggle with the repayments?

High stakes or small stakes?

Assessing your borrowing capacity is a very personal matter. For some people, the thought of going into debt doesn't create any anxiety at all; these people will happily borrow as much as a bank will lend them. Others break into a sweat at the mere thought of borrowing any more than they absolutely have to. This fear might be justified under some circumstances; however, it's often more a consequence of a lack of education, knowledge and experience. In other words, if these people sat down, crunched the numbers and really considered the risks involved, going into debt may not look as daunting as they first thought.

Of course, having said that, you need to be totally comfortable with any debt you take on. The last thing you want to do is borrow more than you can afford and get into trouble down the track. The good news is that lenders (and mortgage brokers) don't want this to happen either. They're in the business of lending money and having it repaid: they really don't want to have to sell your assets to recoup their funds.

The best way for you to come to terms with your borrowing capacity and feel more comfortable about it is to draw up a budget and start to stick to it. Some of you might shudder at the mere thought of having to put your financial habits on paper, but let me assure you that budgeting is the best way to plan ahead. So, let's look at some simple tips and things you should consider when planning and budgeting to buy your next property purchase, funded (at least partly) by a mortgage.

> *We can loan you enough money to get you completely out of debt.* —A bank sign

It's a numbers game

Many people find themselves winging it when they're asked how much money they have coming in and going out each week, fortnight or month. The vast majority of new clients I meet can't tell me with confidence how much they spend – they're willing to guess/estimate, often incorrectly, but they really don't know. Yet, if you have any significant financial commitments, particularly a mortgage, you should be budgeting on a regular basis.

Many people have lost a game of Monopoly due to failing to budget and spending all their money. Budgeting helps you understand exactly where your money goes and allows you to make conscious decisions and plan for the future.

How to work out what you're spending

The simplest way to work out what you're spending is to review the past three months' worth of transaction-account and credit-card statements. Most banks will allow you to download your transactions from internet banking into a spreadsheet.

You then allocate the expense transactions to categories. The seven categories I recommend are:

1. **financial commitments**, such as rent, mortgages, car leases, school fees and child support
2. **utilities**, including costs for gas, electricity, rates, phone, water, internet and contents insurance
3. **health and education**, such as school fees, health insurance, medical expenses and child care
4. **shopping and transport**, like food, clothing, beauty, petrol, car maintenance and public transport expenses
5. **entertainment**, including spending on holidays, gifts, eating out, movies and coffees
6. **cash**, which is all withdrawals from ATMs – if this figure is high, stop using cash and start using EFTPOS or credit cards more often, as this makes tracking your spending much easier. Remember, you can't manage what you can't measure
7. **other**, which is anything that doesn't fit in the preceding categories.

Simple budgeting

The next step is to investigate each of these seven categories to explore if any savings can be made. For example, you may be able to save on non-discretionary (i.e. fixed) expenses such as utilities by switching electricity providers. These are easy savings to make, because they don't impact on your standard of living.

When it comes to discretionary items such as eating out, if you feel you're spending too much, then you need to set a reasonable budget.

Once you've decided how much you'd like to spend in future on 'general living expenses' (that is, categories 4 to 7 above), work out what that amount translates to every month or fortnight, or however often you get paid. Let's assume your general living expenses are $2000 per fortnight.

Then, you need to have two bank accounts:

1. a savings account
2. a spending account.

Have all your income deposited into the saving account, and pay all your expenses from categories 1, 2 and 3 from that account. Set up an automatic transfer of a fixed amount (in this example, $2000) from the savings account into the spending account when you get paid, and use this to pay for expenses in categories 4 to 7.

If the spending account's balance hits zero, you've run out of money. Stop spending! This structure will help you keep on track without needing to count every cent.

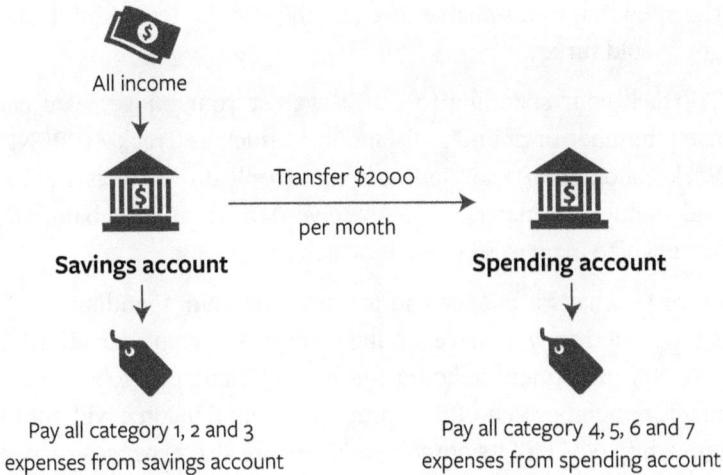

All income

Savings account → Transfer $2000 per month → Spending account

Pay all category 1, 2 and 3 expenses from savings account

Pay all category 4, 5, 6 and 7 expenses from spending account

The reason category 1, 2 and 3 expenses are paid from the savings account is that they're relatively fixed, non-discretionary expenses. People rarely overspend in these categories. The categories that need the most attention and discipline are 4 to 7.

Reining in spending

Be realistic when setting your budget. Remember that old adage 'Failing to plan is planning to fail'? Well, when you draw up your budget, failing to plan within the realms of reality will most certainly set you up to fail. So, make sure that your income will cover whatever you plan to spend and, on the other side of the coin, don't budget too little. If you resolve to live on only a few dollars each week, you'll end up throwing your budget out the window and deciding it's all too hard.

You need to take a long, hard and honest look at yourself and your spending habits, however. If you have a tendency to overindulge – treating yourself often to new clothes or eating out regularly, for example – make sure that your indulgences are accurately recorded when you calculate your current expenses, and plan in your budget to curb this spending. I recommend slowly reducing the spending to a sensible level, as this will be less painful than going cold turkey.

To track your spending to check against your budget, you can use a number of online tools and apps, such as TrackMySPEND, Pocketbook and PocketSmith, to name only a few. Most are free and highly automated – they receive data from your bank and learn which expenses belong in which categories.

Once you have a budget and are tracking your spending, you'll know whether you have enough surplus income to afford a property investment or home purchase. With respect to an investment, remember that often a property's rental income will not be enough to cover all its outgoings. There are also expenses such as maintenance and repair costs that come up on an irregular basis and which you'll need to allow for in your budget.

If you'd like more information about cash-flow-management tactics, I have written several blog posts that are available online, and have a whole chapter on this topic in my book *Investopoly*.

*My problem lies in reconciling my gross habits with
my net income.* —Errol Flynn

Playing devil's advocate

When looking at your budget to assess how much you should borrow, make sure you always consider the worst-case scenario. Plan for the worst and hope for the best! On the income side, be conservative. Don't count on receiving bonuses from your employer, for example, unless you have a history of consistently receiving these. Don't overestimate rental income from any property investments and remember to factor in vacancy rates and expenses.

On the expenses side, overestimate. After budgeting for a while, you'll get to know your average monthly spending, but always include a buffer for unexpected costs, as these can and will crop up, particularly if you own an investment property.

When it comes to interest rates on your property loans, make sure you build in a safety margin. I normally recommend preparing a budget using a 6 to 6.5 per cent interest rate, and your investment still needs to be affordable at 7 per cent even if it's a bit of a stretch. Interest rates are at all-time lows at the time of writing in 2020, and are expected to be low for maybe the next five or more years; however, at some point they'll increase and you must ensure that you can afford it.

If your budget is very sensitive to interest-rate movements (that is, if you won't have a large surplus income after taking into account the mortgage repayments), then it might be worthwhile to consider choosing or switching to a fixed-rate mortgage, or reducing your loan (which we'll discuss more in chapter 3), or both.

Making a back-up plan

Occasionally Plan A can go a little pear-shaped, so it's important to have something up your sleeve in the form of a Plan B. As much as you don't want to think about scary prospects such as losing your job or succumbing to prolonged illness, these events can and do occur.

Plan B might involve accessing emergency funds you've stashed away, making sure you have adequate insurance (such as income-protection insurance, which is a must-have for most borrowers), drawing down on a loan facility or even selling some liquid assets such as shares. If you don't have a solid, workable Plan B, then maybe it's not the right time for you to be thinking about borrowing more money.

Polishing the crystal ball

It would be nice if we all had a crystal ball, and it can be difficult to predict what's around the corner without one, but it's important to consider the future nonetheless when budgeting. People's income and expenses can change dramatically over time.

At different stages of our lives, different expenses arise. Starting a family is probably one of the most significant changes that will happen to many of us, and often it's a double whammy. One wage-earner may take a break from the workforce, either temporarily or permanently, resulting in a lower household income, while at the same time your cost of living increases. Have a think about the foreseeable future and take life-changing events such as this into consideration.

Planning at least five years in advance is a good idea; undertaking detailed planning and budgeting will often give you more confidence and reduce stress levels. For example, if you've budgeted for at least a 2 per cent interest-rate rise, you'll no longer be uneasy when there's talk of increases – comfortable in the knowledge that you'll be able to cope.

Improving your cash-flow management really doesn't take much time if you set up your banking correctly, as described earlier, and it costs nothing. However, poor cash-flow management will cost you dearly!

PLAYING TO WIN

Control your cash flow, don't let cash flow control you! Good cash-flow management is paramount if you have one or more mortgages. Make sure you track how much you're spending and structure your bank accounts to avoid unconscious overspending.

Counting your chips

Once you have a better handle on your budget and how much surplus cash flow you have, you'll be in a perfect position to undertake some planning. Of course, when planning, you need to consider any potential changes to that cash flow over the short to medium term.

Let's assume your surplus cash flow is $20,000 per annum and that you want to invest in a property. How much should you borrow? Here's a simple calculation to work out what size loan $20,000 per year will service, at two different interest rates:

Item	Notes	At 4%	At 6.5%
Property value		$750,000	$750,000
Rental income	4% of property value	$30,000	$30,000
Property expenses	25% of gross rental	-$7,500	-$7,500
Interest	Based on total borrowings of $787,500* which includes costs (stamp duty)	-$31,500	-$51,200

* See chapter 5 for a description of how to structure the loans to borrow the total cost of the property.

Item	Notes	At 4%	At 6.5%
Pre-tax loss		–$9,000	–$28,700
Tax saving	Assuming marginal tax rate is 39%	$3,500	$11,200
Post-tax cost	**Actual cash flow cost**	–$5,500	–$17,500

As you can see, investing in a property worth $750,000 appears to be very comfortable. At a 4 per cent interest rate, it will cost $9,000 per annum before tax and $5,500 after tax (the tax saving results from negative gearing, which I discuss in chapter 7). Even if interest rates increased to 6.5 per cent it would still be affordable, as the after-tax cost is less than your $20,000 surplus.

Becoming borrower-ready

Over the six months before you plan to submit a loan application, there are a few things you may need to work on. Given how much credit has tightened over recent years (as discussed in chapter 1), it's very important to take proactive steps so that you can present the strongest possible application. Following are a few things you may like to consider.

STEPS TO A STRONG LOAN APPLICATION

Minimise your discretionary spending six months prior to lodging an application. Lenders will review your transaction accounts and credit-card statements to verify how much you spend, and typically won't distinguish between discretionary and non-discretionary expenses. Also, if you've spent a lot in a discretionary category such as eating out in a particular month, they'll assume you'll do so every month. Of course, this isn't common sense – and arguably eating out a lot provides strong evidence that you do have surplus cash flow. Very few people would prioritise eating out before loan repayments! In any case, reducing your expenditure to an absolute minimum provides four benefits. It will:

1. demonstrate to the bank that you have enough surplus cash flow to make loan repayments

2. prevent intrusive and possibly insulting interrogation about how and why you spend your money

3. reveal the minimum amount of money you need to maintain a basic but satisfactory standard of living, which will help with your planning and also provide a basis for the disclosure (listing) of living expenses in the application form

4. maximise your savings.

Close any accounts and credit cards that you don't use. As I'll explain in chapter 3, credit-card limits reduce your borrowing capacity.

Think about any career and job changes in advance. Changing employment a few months prior to lodging a mortgage application isn't a good strategy.

If you have existing mortgages, consider restructuring. Lenders' assessment of your borrowing capacity can vary a lot. One way to extend your borrowing capacity is to move your loans onto one or two securities (properties). This may free up a property that you can take to a new lender that has a much higher borrowing capacity. A mortgage broker who specialises in advising investors will be able to advise you about restructuring strategies.

Make sure that all financial dealings are conducted perfectly – all loans, credit cards and bills paid on time, and so on. Even a small oversight can have a negative impact on your borrowing capacity.

Establish a relationship with the one or two banks that you may want to borrow from, to build a credit history with them. If you're an existing customer, you'll be regarded as a lower risk. I discuss the benefits of using various institutions in chapter 4.

Make sure that your taxation affairs are up to date, and any associated liabilities have been paid. Lodge any overdue tax returns.

Repay any consumer debt (e.g. personal loans, car leases), if possible. Typically, the repayments on unsecured loans are proportionally a lot higher than mortgages, and substantially reduce your borrowing capacity.

Meet with a professional mortgage broker (or lender, if you know which institution you'll use) and discuss your situation. They may be able to share ideas and tips specific to your situation that will help you maximise the likelihood of a loan being approved.

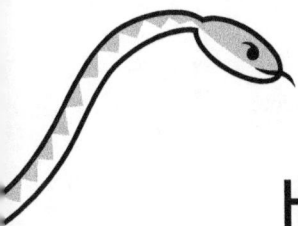

3.

HOW MUCH CAN YOU BORROW?

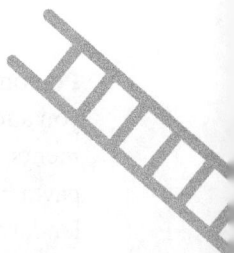

Now that we've discussed how to assess what your comfortable borrowing capacity is and how to prepare for a loan application, let's look at the lender's calculation – 'the rules of the lending game'. For a lender, your borrowing capacity hinges on three key criteria:

1. income and expenses, known as 'serviceability'
2. assets and liabilities, known as 'security'
3. borrowing history, referred to as 'creditworthiness'.

Serviceability

For obvious reasons, the first thing a lender will consider when you apply for a loan is whether you earn enough money to comfortably repay it. You don't have to be making millions to start investing, but your income needs to cover the prospective loan repayments, your living expenses and any other financial commitments.

In other words, you need to demonstrate to the lender that you will have enough money to cover all your expenses, with a small amount left over as a buffer.

If you're borrowing to purchase an investment property, lenders will generally use this simple formula:

$$\begin{aligned} &\quad \text{Income after tax} \\ -\ &\text{Personal financial commitments} \\ +\ &\text{Rental income} \\ -\ &\text{Loan repayments} \\ =\ &\text{Must be surplus income} \end{aligned}$$

Personal financial commitments include living expenses for you and your family, as well as rent or existing home-loan repayments, credit cards and personal-loan repayments, child-support payments, car leases and so forth. The surplus will reassure the lender that if your income temporarily changes or interest rates rise, you'll still have the capacity to meet the loan repayments.

Be aware that credit cards can reduce your borrowing capacity even if the balance is zero. This is because lenders will calculate your capacity based on a worst-case scenario in which your credit card is fully utilised. They'll assume the monthly repayment is equal to 3.8 per cent of the card's credit limit. So, for example, if you have a card with a $10,000 credit limit, the lender will assume that this will cost you $380 per month in repayments.

Rental income will be 'shaded', meaning that the lender will only include a percentage of the gross estimated rental income. This is normally in the range of 70 to 80 per cent, with the average gross rental income used for the assessment being generally around 80 per cent. This is done to account for the expenses associated with owning an investment property (e.g. property management and maintenance costs) and the vacancy risk.

Loan repayments will be calculated as the dollar value of principal and interest repayments using a benchmark interest rate (which is a fixed margin of at least 2.5 per cent above the loan's actual rate), regardless of how you elect to structure the loan repayments. The lender will then compare this amount to the assessed rental income.

At the time of writing this book, benchmark interest rates typically range from 5.35 to 5.75 per cent. To demonstrate how this works, let's look at an example.

Example

Assume a property is valued at $500,000 with a rental yield of 4 per cent. The investor borrowed 80 per cent of the property's value in order to acquire it, or $400,000.

The assessed rental income would be equal to, say, 80 per cent of the estimated 4 per cent yield – as 80 per cent is the average gross rental income lenders will generally use. That's $500,000 × 4 per cent × 80 per cent, which equals $16,000 per annum.

This would be compared to the assessed principal and interest repayments on the $400,000 loan at the benchmark rate of, say, 5.75 per cent, which equals $30,200 per annum. (That's over a 25-year term, assuming that the total loan term is 30 years, with the first 5 years interest-only and the remaining 25 years principal-and-interest.)

Therefore, the applicant must have surplus income of at least $14,200 per annum (being $16,000 less $30,200) to qualify for this loan.

However, in reality, if the loan is interest-only, the rental income will come very close to covering the repayments, thereby costing very little.

What if the property's actual cash flow is neutral?

You will note that based on the lender's assessment, the property produces a negative cash flow – that is, the loan repayments are a lot more than the net rental income. This is very common. As such, from a lender's point of view, every investment property you purchase eats into your borrowing capacity – even if the actual cash flow is neutral.

A property would need to have a gross rental yield of more than 7.5 per cent for it to have a neutral effect on your borrowing capacity (if you're borrowing 80 per cent), and it's very uncommon for residential property yields to be above 5.5 per cent. Be very sceptical, therefore, if someone suggests that it's easy to acquire a large number of properties in a short space of time. Each property will 'eat' into your borrowing capacity, so unless you have a substantial income, you'll exhaust that capacity pretty quickly. This is still the case even if the property portfolio's actual cash flow is positive.

Lenders' assessments are conservative, but not without reason. Always consider your interest rate exposure and the effect a rental market downturn would have on your position. You need to have a sufficient buffer to weather a shrinking rental market.

Example

The following table sets out an example of how a lender will assess an application.

Item	Description	Example
Employment income	The bank will verify your income from the year-to-date (YTD) income on your pay slip. They won't always include 100% of bonuses, commission or any 'at risk' income. If you're self-employed, lenders will typically review the past two years of your financial results and make adjustments for items such as depreciation, salaries paid to you and associates, and so on.	Rick and Karen are both employed. Rick's salary is $250,000 and Karen works part-time, earning $80,000. Their monthly after-tax income is $18,347.

Item	Description	Example
Rental income	Most lenders will include 70 to 80% of gross rental income to allow for expenses.	Rick owns an investment property and the tenant pays $505 per week. The lender includes $1531 of monthly income.
Living expenses	This is where the fun begins. The lender will review the last three months of your bank statements to ascertain what you spend.	Rick and Karen have stated that they spend $8,000 per month.
Credit cards	Most banks will multiply your credit-card limits by 3.8% to work out the minimum repayment if your card was fully drawn.	Rick and Karen have $15,000 of credit-card limits, so a monthly expense of $570 is added.
Mortgages	Repayments are worked out using a benchmark interest rate on a principal and interest (P&I) basis.	Rick and Karen have two loans: a home loan for $850,000 and an investment loan for $750,000. Monthly repayments over 25 years at 7.25% are $10,914.
Result	Total income must be greater than total expenses.	Total income is $19,878. Total expenses are $19,484. The surplus is $394. Rick and Karen wouldn't qualify for any additional borrowings.

Security

'Security' refers to how much cash you'll contribute to acquisition costs and/or how much equity in other property you can offer to secure a loan. Essentially, if you default on the loan's repayments, the lender wants to have enough security (asset) to sell that they'd be able to recover their monies.

Security is important from a creditworthiness perspective, because it demonstrates that you have 'skin in the game' – that is, that your assets are on the line and you have something to lose if you stop making the loan repayments. If you didn't have equity on the line, you might just walk away if it all got too hard.

Most investors prefer to limit their loans to no more than 80 per cent (per property) of the current value of each property. One reason for this is to ensure that they don't have to pay lenders mortgage insurance (LMI). As discussed in chapter 1, LMI is a one-off cost that borrowers must pay at the beginning of the loan when they borrow at a certain loan-to-valuation ratio (LVR). LMI insures the lender's risk should they ever have to repossess and sell the property but there's a shortfall between the sale proceeds and the loan amount.

Mortgage insurance can cost between 1 and 5 per cent of the loan amount: it may not seem like much, but it can be a substantial chunk if you're borrowing a large amount of money. Another drawback of LMI is a mortgage insurer has to approve your application, as well as the lender. (Again, chapter 1 has more detail on this.)

Most mortgage insurance companies will consider lending up to 95 per cent of a property's value, typically up to a maximum loan amount of $750,000. The next level down is 90 per cent loans: most insurers will lend up to 90 per cent of the property's value up to a maximum loan amount of $1 million. Prior to the GFC, these LVRs and loan amounts were higher – borrowers used to be able to borrow 100 per cent including LMI. Those days are gone now.

Some lenders, however, allow you to add the cost of mortgage insurance onto the loan over and above 95 per cent – up to a maximum of 97 per cent. For example, if the mortgage insurance cost 3.5 per cent, you could add 2 per cent to the loan (being a loan for 97 per cent) and pay the remaining 1.50 per cent from your cash holdings.

You really need to assess the pros and cons of purchasing earlier by borrowing more than 80 per cent and paying for LMI, versus delaying the purchase so you can save more and avoid LMI. In a fast-rising property market, the cost of mortgage insurance can quickly be offset by capital appreciation, assuming the property delivers the capital gains you expect and your financial circumstances are strong enough to support the borrowings.

For some property types, on the other hand, lenders will restrict the LVR and won't always lend 80 per cent. I've provided a summary of credit policies in the appendix to this book.

Generally, security, not serviceability, is the biggest hurdle to getting into the property market. Once you're in the market, it all comes down to holding the right properties (ones that grow in value) and being patient while you wait for their value to increase.

Are you genuine?

If you want to borrow more than 90 per cent of a property's value, you'll generally need to demonstrate that out of your deposit, at least 5 per cent of the property's value is 'genuine savings'.

'Genuine savings' are the result of a demonstrable savings pattern in the name of at least one borrower, over a minimum period of three months prior to the loan application being received. Any lump-sum cash injections, such as gifts from immediate family members, must have been held in an account in the name of at least one borrower for a minimum of three months prior to the application to count towards genuine savings.

Your ability to accumulate genuine savings gives the lender comfort that you have surplus income and aren't spending everything you earn. It reassures them that you can afford the repayments – which is particularly important for first-time borrowers.

Of course, if you already own a property, genuine savings can be replaced by equity – the value of your existing property less any existing liabilities.

Borrowing history

Your borrowing history can come back to bite you, if you're not careful! A good borrowing history means that you've paid your bills and past loan commitments on time without getting any black marks, in the form of defaults appearing on your credit report.

Your borrowing history tells a lender about your creditworthiness and your willingness to repay a loan. Some people regard a mortgage as an extremely important commitment and would never even get close to missing a payment. Other people are too relaxed about such matters, taking the approach that they'll get around to making payments in their own time. Lenders want to lend to the former and avoid the latter.

Prior to March 2014, Australian credit-reporting agencies only recorded negative information about borrowers: the number of credit applications made, any defaults on loan repayments, bankruptcy and so on. As such, credit reports used to provide very little information to help banks assess whether a borrower represented a good or bad risk.

However, since 1 July 2019, the government has mandated that lenders must provide all the positive credit data they have to reporting agencies. This includes data about things like whether you have made all loan repayments on time, information about current accounts held, what credit contracts you've successfully repaid in full, accounts that you've opened and closed and so on. It paints a better picture of your creditworthiness.

Lenders use this information to generate a credit score for you: a statistical assessment of your creditworthiness. In the past, you maintained a good credit score simply by staying out of trouble: that is, by not defaulting. However, now, with positive credit data, you can improve your credit record by making sure you keep on top of your finances – paying bills on time, not overdrawing your accounts, keeping credit applications to a minimum, keeping credit card balances low and so on.

Sometimes, people are enticed to apply for credit cards simply to qualify for incentives like frequent flyer points, and cancel the card once they've collected the incentive. However, be very careful with these sorts of activities, as they can damage your credit score.

It's worth checking your credit rating before you apply for a loan, to avoid nasty surprises. Occasionally, too, mistakes can occur and it's better to have these corrected before lenders see them and start asking questions. To find out how to obtain a free copy of your credit file and what to do if there are errors, go to the Australian Securities & Investments Commission's (ASIC's) MoneySmart website (www.moneysmart.gov.au) and search for the term 'credit reports'. The site has lots of useful information and links.

PLAYING TO WIN

Optimise your creditworthiness by keeping on top of the information recorded on your credit file. Pay all bills on time. Keep credit-card limits low. Keep credit enquiries to a minimum. Focus on building a good credit history.

Different lenders, different borrowing capacities

I explained earlier how borrowing capacity is calculated. Bear in mind that this is a generalisation, however, and the reality is that each lender has its own idiosyncrasies with respect to credit policies. Sometimes, different lenders may assess your borrowing capacity dramatically differently – some lenders suit different types of borrowers better.

So, as we discussed in chapter 1, it's important to consider various lenders. Better still, you could employ a mortgage broker to compare your borrowing capacity with over 30 lenders in one fell swoop, saving you time and ensuring you don't miss opportunities.

Building your borrowing capacity

It's vital to *always* ensure that you're borrowing within your personal means. Don't be tempted to borrow to the hilt because a finance company or bank says you can. Set aside the lender's borrowing capacity calculations and work out your own budget, so you know you're choosing a comfortable level of debt exposure. As discussed in chapter 2, make sure that you consider the impact of potential interest-rate rises on your financial health, too.

Having said that, there's nothing wrong with trying to increase your borrowing capacity, within reason, as long as you maintain a sensible level of personal debt that you can service without stress.

Here are some handy hints on how to increase your borrowing capacity:

- **Minimise credit-card limits.** Even if you repay your credit cards in full every month, a lender will allow for their full utilisation when calculating your borrowing capacity. This means that even $10,000 of limits can reduce your borrowing capacity by approximately $65,000. Keep your limits as low as possible and/or use Visa Debit cards instead.

- **Apply for the longest loan term possible.** This will keep your minimum repayments as low as possible on existing loans. In particular, avoid short-term car leases with large monthly repayments.

- **Select interest-only repayments on existing loans.** This is another way to keep minimum repayments low.

- **Review rental income.** Constantly review the rental income from any investment properties you have, and increase rents wherever possible. Sometimes making cosmetic improvements to the property can allow you to charge a higher rent.

- **Submit a PAYG tax variation to your employer.** This reduces the amount of tax deducted from your wage, so that you receive more income through the year, instead of getting a lump sum refund at tax time. You can do this if you expect to be able to claim a negative gearing taxation benefit.

- **Prepare a budget.** Some lenders will be impressed if you present an accurate budget that sets out your real cash flow position (i.e. income and expenses) and which demonstrates that you can afford to take on more debt. They may take this into account and ignore the fact that you may not meet their 'standard' serviceability criteria, although this is becoming rarer. Note any mitigating factors like income-protection insurance, rental insurance or continuity of tenancy.

- **Maximise non-cash tax deductions to reduce your tax bill.** In other words, ensure that you're claiming any depreciation benefits you're entitled to.

- **Maximise property valuations.** Chapter 9 has details on how to do this.

- **Maintain good records of investment income.** By recording all interest and dividends, you can demonstrate to the bank that you receive this income on a regular basis. Most lenders will need at least two years of history for this type of income.

- **Ask for a pay rise!** There's no harm in trying to increase your salary.
- **Put off starting a family.** Consider family planning issues and how they'll affect your borrowing capacity. It might be easier to borrow money while you have no financial dependants (children).
- **Rent out a room in your home to generate extra income.** Lenders will want to see consistency of this income in your tax return: 12 to 24 months of evidence would be required. Not all lenders will take this into account, however.
- **Share your rental accommodation.** If you don't own your home, getting in a flatmate will reduce your monthly rental expense.

A mortgage broker will be able to review your financial situation and offer you advice that's specific to your circumstances to help you maximise your borrowing capacity.

What should you do if you start to struggle?

Even if you're careful to create a budget and plan your borrowings to limit the risk of getting into debt over your head, sometimes things happen in life to change your financial position.

If this happens to you, I can't stress enough how important it is to take immediate action as soon as you realise that you're having difficulties meeting loan repayment obligations. Ignoring the issue in the hope that it'll go away, or that the lender won't notice, will only make it more difficult to deal with in the long run. There's nothing wrong with admitting you're having problems; and if you take action quickly, a simple solution or arrangement can probably be put in place.

First, you need to understand why you're having difficulties. Ask yourself what's changed: is it your income? Rent payments? Expenses? Are the changes permanent or temporary?

If your expenses are the issue, then it's time to identify areas in which you can cut costs. Reanalyse your budget (as detailed in chapter 2) and compare it against your actual expenses to see where you're overspending.

If income is the problem, is the setback something permanent or temporary? If it's a short-term hiccup, you might have to dip into your emergency money – that's what it's there for. However, if you conclude that the income reduction is permanent, you may have to take alternative action.

Over the next few pages, I explain things you can consider doing if you find yourself struggling to keep up with loan commitments.

Contact the lender

Discuss your concerns with your lender and try to come up with a way to work through the difficulties you're experiencing. One possible solution might be a repayment holiday (a period in which you're not required to make repayments), although this is normally only available if you're in advance with your repayments.

Some people feel reluctant to tell the lender about their issues, fearing that they might sell the property from under them. In reality, lenders prefer to do anything but sell the property. A forced sale is time-consuming, costly and simply not good business – lenders would prefer to keep on charging you interest into the foreseeable future. So, don't be scared to share! It's in their interest to help you out wherever possible.

Reset your mortgage term

Let's say that you took out a $400,000 (30-year) mortgage five years ago, and the balance is now $350,000. What you could do is reset the existing balance (of $350,000) over 30 years again, thereby reducing your minimum repayments. This would cut repayments by approximately $240 per month, based on an interest rate of 4 per cent.

Switch to interest-only

Another alternative is to request a short interest-only term: say, 12 months. Most interest-only loans allow principal repayments at any time. This gives you the flexibility of choosing to make lower monthly repayments by repaying interest only or opt to pay interest and principal (whatever you can afford).

Be aware, however, that many banks are reluctant to offer interest-only repayments for owner-occupier home loans. Also, switching from principal and interest to interest-only repayments will require you to submit an application. If your financial situation has deteriorated, such an application may not be approved.

Reduce expenditure

Try to cut down on any surplus expenses. This comes back to budgeting and having a good understanding of where your money is going.

Consolidate debts

Consolidating debts (for example, by extending your mortgage to pay off all other personal loans or credit-card debt) can reduce your overall monthly repayment commitments, and often the effective interest rate, too. However, consolidating debts into a mortgage may actually end up costing you more in interest in the long run, since the debt is repaid over a longer term than an unsecured loan (30 years as opposed to 5 years).

Increase your income

Consider taking on a second job to earn some additional income, or asking your boss for a salary review. Working a second job may be difficult, especially if you have a young family, but you might be able to come up with ways to earn extra income from home.

Seek help

If you have problems managing your finances, don't be afraid to ask for help from a specialist financial counsellor. They might be able to suggest solutions that you hadn't thought of.

* * *

Most of these solutions are temporary fixes, and should only be used if you don't expect to experience repayment difficulties on an ongoing basis. If your financial situation has changed permanently, though, you may need to consider selling one of your properties or to come up with some other method of reducing your debts.

If you're simply in over your head and need a way out, face up to it. Hanging on stubbornly will only impair your financial security now and in the future.

> *Th' safest way t' double your money is t' fold it over once an' put it back in your pocket.*
> —Kin Hubbard (in *Abe Martin*)

What will the bank do?

As I've mentioned, if you get into financial trouble, the banks will be as reluctant as you to force you to sell up and cut your losses. It's in their best interest not to sell a property when a client starts to struggle with repayments.

The bank would prefer not to have to take possession of your property and put it on the market – not because they have an emotional interest in it like you, but because selling will eat up a lot of time and money. This will, therefore, be a lender's absolute last resort.

Their actions will depend on the individual circumstances and may vary from bank to bank, with the entire process normally taking several months. Here's an overview of the steps they might consider before it comes to the final crunch:

- If a repayment isn't made on time, the bank will issue you with a letter – for home loans, they're required to do this by law. The letter will simply state that the repayment is required within a certain time frame.

- If the repayment isn't made within this time frame (say, 30 days), then the bank will contact you and attempt to find a solution. This may involve taking a number of steps, such as resetting the loan term or providing a repayment holiday if you're experiencing temporary financial difficulty.

- If you can't agree on a solution or if the bank hasn't been able to make contact with you within a couple of months, then the file is transferred to its legal area (or external lawyers) to manage the loan and comply with legal requirements, including issuing letters of default. The default will be recorded on your personal credit file.

- At this point, you have two options. You can refinance the loan (normally using a non-conforming lender, since you're in default) or sell the property and pay out the loan. You have approximately 30 days to make this decision.

Borrowers are normally encouraged to investigate both of these options themselves, as they have more control of their financial outcome. These days it's a lot easier to refinance a loan, as there are lenders that specialise in assisting borrowers in default (i.e. non-conforming lenders). However, they'll charge approximately 1 per cent to 2 per cent more than the standard variable interest rate.

The alternative is to sell up and cut your losses. This may seem a harrowing prospect, but you're always better off retaining control and putting your property on the market before the lender does, as it's unclear whether lenders have a duty of care to the borrower when exercising their power to sell a property. In other words, they may not have an obligation to act in your best interest.

If you can't repay the loan through a refinance or sale, as a last resort the bank will take possession of the property and engage a real estate agent to sell it, after issuing the relevant notices. The law sets out three conditions that must be met before a lender can take possession and sell your property:

1. There must be a default (either through non-repayment of principal or interest or through not fulfilling another provision contained in the mortgage contract).
2. A notice must be served to the mortgagor requesting that the default be remedied (for example, by repayment of overdue amounts). The mortgage documents will set out how the notice is to be served.
3. The default must continue without remedy for a period of 30 days or one calendar month from the service of the notice.

Generally, lenders will work with you for many months before they decide to take the drastic step of selling your property.

Beyond the numbers game

When you decide to borrow money, you need to do more than just crunch the numbers. First and foremost, you must feel comfortable that you can afford the extra debt, or you could spend many sleepless nights worrying about making your repayments. Listen to your head and your instincts, and seek professional advice. Borrowing tolerance is a very personal thing, so don't allow yourself to be bullied into borrowing more, unless the bully is also offering to repay the loan for you!

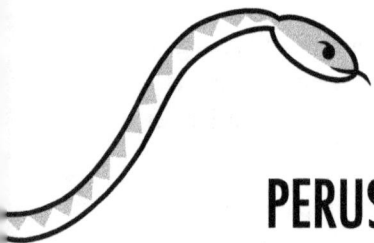

4.

PERUSING THE PRODUCTS

In this chapter, we'll look at the mortgage products on offer, to give you an overview. Bear in mind, however, that you should first determine what loan structure will best help you achieve your goals – which is the topic of the next two chapters – and then choose the products accordingly, not the other way around.

When borrowers make mistakes, nine times out of ten it's because they've selected the wrong product – rather than the wrong lender. Most lenders offer the same suite of products, with slight variations according to their credit policies and criteria, so choosing a product that isn't well suited to your individual circumstances and requirements may have a greater financial impact than signing up with the wrong bank. Decide which structure and product is best for you, then consider which lender offers the best deal for that particular product.

The more alternatives, the more difficult the choice.
—Abbe' D'Allanival

Keep it simple

It might seem as if there's a plethora of mortgage products out there, as lenders come up with fancy labels and marketing ploys to grab your attention. Essentially, though, there are six main product categories to choose from:

1. discount variable loans
2. basic variable loans
3. standard variable loans
4. packages
5. fixed rate loans
6. lines of credit
7. offset accounts (normally linked to a standard variable loan).

Which is the right one for you? Let's examine each individually to determine the circumstances in which a particular mortgage product should be used and find out which might suit you best.

Discount variable loans

Generally, discount variable loan products offer a discounted interest rate for the first 12 months, then revert to a higher interest rate. Don't be tempted by this little carrot: the lender is aiming to entice you into the loan with a low 'honeymoon' rate and then slug you with the cold, hard reality of a higher rate afterward.

Remember, your goal should be to attain the lowest ongoing costs. One year of supposed generosity doesn't cut it if you spend the next 25 to 29 years paying the lender's (high) standard rate.

On top of this, some discount variable products have high exit fees. If you try to refinance or switch to an alternative product after the initial discounted rate has expired, you may be liable for significant fees. This has the effect of locking you into an uncompetitive loan.

The volume of introductory rate products has dramatically reduced over the past decade, probably as a result of the government's tighter regulation of when and how lenders can change exit fees. Some lenders used to charge really exorbitant fees, but this is no longer allowed. I also suspect that the Australian public has wised up to these marketing tricks. Put simply, introductory rate products are unlikely to be appropriate for most borrowers.

I'd only recommend that you consider using a discount variable loan if you intend to hold the property for a short period of time – say, for one year. If you do plan to purchase and dispose of a property quickly, this could be the best loan product. Look for a loan that has minimal or no break costs (there are some around) and take advantage of that cheaper honeymoon rate for the first 12 months.

Basic variable loans

Most lenders offer a basic variable loan as a no-frills product with minimal features. Some example of features that you may forgo include:

- interest-only repayments – this can be a negative for investors, particularly
- offset accounts, which I'll discuss later in this chapter
- redraw facilities – or there may be higher fees for redrawing.

A 'redraw' is when you withdraw money from your loan, where you've repaid more than the minimum repayments. Many loan products allow you to withdraw your extra repayments at any time.

Basic variable products often have an application fee, typically around $600, and ongoing monthly fees which are usually in the range of $5 and $15. Some basic variables also have higher exit fees (fees you pay if you refinance or repay the loan), so it's good to check this.

However, interest rates for basic variable products are lower than the bank standard variable rate, usually by between 1.50 per cent and 1.80 per cent. Sometimes lenders will offer 'special' interest rate discounts for a limited time.

This type of product is best suited to borrowers who only have one loan and don't expect to need to change their banking structure in the short to medium term. This would typically include, for example, an owner-occupier who does not expect to borrow to invest and simply wants to repay their mortgage as fast as possible.

Standard variable loans

Most standard variable loan products are fully featured: they have all the bells and whistles. However, no borrower should ever pay the standard variable interest rate! The only time I'd recommend a standard variable product is when it's in a package... which is a great segue into the next section.

Packages

More than a decade ago, 'packages' were only offered to certain professionals, and weren't even advertised; that's why they're commonly referred to as 'professional packages'. However, today, they're commonplace, especially with large lenders (banks), and are no longer restricted to specific professions.

A package typically has the following features:

- It offers variable and fixed-rate discounts based on your overall borrowings and loan limits. Many lenders offer 'standard' discounts as well as unadvertised discounts: that is, they'll offer higher discounts to retain or win your business. I discuss negotiating interest-rate discounts later in this chapter.

- Instead of paying application and monthly fees, the lender will charge you one annual fee – typically between $350 and $450 per year. This fee allows you to establish multiple new mortgages, switch between products, request your properties be revalued at no cost, and so on.
- Often, packages include a free credit card and transaction account. It used to be that these were mandatory; however, as a result of the Royal Commission in 2018, many lenders no longer 'force' these products, particularly the credit cards, on borrowers.

A package is a good solution for anyone with more than one mortgage, particularly investors. They allow a borrower to manage and utilise the equity in multiple properties efficiently, while minimising the overall cost of debt. If you are (or plan to become) an investor, it's likely that a package is a suitable product for you.

Fixed loans

Fixed loans are pretty straightforward. Essentially, as the name suggests, the interest rate is fixed for a specific period. Normally, you have the option of choosing a fixed-rate period of one, two, three, four, five, seven or ten years. Only a handful of lenders offer fixed terms longer than five years, though, as these aren't very popular with Australian borrowers.

There are three key restrictions with fixed-rate products:

1. Generally, there's a limit on the extra repayments you can make over and above the minimum repayments. Most lenders restrict extra repayments to $10,000 per year; sometimes they limit the total extra repayments over the fixed-rate term to, say, between $20,000 and $30,000. It's wise to ascertain this from the outset.

2. Almost no lenders allow an offset account to be linked to a fixed rate loan. (We'll look at offset accounts later on in this chapter.)

3. If you refinance or pay out a fixed-rate product before the fixed term is finished, you may have to pay substantial break fees. These fees are tied to interest rate movements, and so are unascertainable at the time you take out the loan. Perhaps this is best explained using an example. Let's say that John takes out a fixed-rate loan in January 2020 for $100,000, fixed for five years at 5 per cent per annum. Assume that he sells the property a year later, in January 2021, with four years remaining on the fixed term, and repays the loan. If the four-year fixed rates were to have fallen to, say, 3 per cent per annum at that time, then the bank would charge John a fee equal to 2 per cent per annum – 5 per cent minus the 3 per cent – for the remaining term of four years. This amount represents the bank's loss: how much John would have paid them minus what they can re-lend the money for now. Fixed-rate break-fee calculations can vary dramatically, however, and, in my opinion, there really isn't enough government regulation and oversight over these fees. In simple terms, if fixed and variable rates fall after your loan is established, you're likely to have to pay a substantial fee. If fixed and variable rates rise after you take out your loan, it may be that no break fees will apply.

There are two reasons borrowers may be attracted to fixed rates. Firstly, they may want repayment certainty – they don't want their cash flow to suffer if interest rates rise after they take out the loan. If your cash flow is tight and interest-rate rises would cause you financial stress, then fixing your rate may be a good solution. Some borrowers select fixed-rate products even if the fixed interest rates are higher than current variable rates, viewing it as the cost of 'insuring' against future variable-rate hikes.

Secondly, borrowers are attracted to fixed rates because they think they'll be financially better off. In the main, I would caution borrowers about this assumption. Fixed rates are set by the money markets, and the money markets are shaped by many participants, including large institutions and governments all around the world. The current prices (the interest rates) reflect these participants' views on future interest rate movements. So, if you feel fixed rates represent value, you're essentially taking the opposite view to 'the market', which won't always be a good idea.

However, there's one additional consideration to weigh up: whether the banks will set their interest rates independently of the Reserve Bank of Australia (RBA), which they began doing after the GFC. For example, say that the market is expecting the RBA to cut variable interest rates, but you believe that the banks won't pass on any reductions, then maybe, the fixed rate could be attractive.

THE RESERVE BANK AND INTEREST RATES

The RBA sets the 'cash rate': the interest rate that the banks charge each other on an overnight basis. This determines a bank's borrowing costs, which directly impacts how much it charges customers. The RBA's goal is to maintain Australia's inflation rate between 2 and 3 per cent per annum. It does this by changing the cash rate, which will change the amount of money in the economy. If rates fall, borrowers pay less interest, so they have more money to spend, which stimulates the economy and hopefully inflation (and vice versa).

The following chart shows whether borrowers who fixed their mortgage interest rate for three years during the period from the year 2000 to the end of 2016 were subsequently financially better or worse off. (The data doesn't go beyond the end of 2016 because, at the time of writing, any three-year fixed term entered into after this point has not yet matured. However, the data is suggesting that anyone who fixed their rate after the end of 2016 will likely be worse off.)

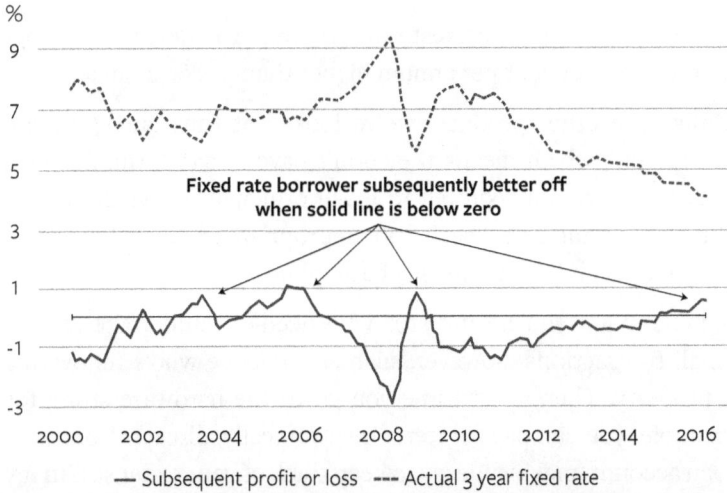

Source: 2020 Reserve Bank of Australia. Reproduced by permission of the Reserve Bank of Australia.

The dotted line is the three-year fixed rate over time. The solid line reflects whether the fixed-rate borrower ended up in profit or loss. When the solid line is above zero, fixed-rate borrowers were better off than if they'd stuck with a variable-rate product. You'll note that the solid line doesn't rise above zero a great deal – only 31 per cent of the time, in fact. This means that 69 per cent of the time, fixed-rate borrowers have been worse off.

So, unless you're worried about cash flow and interest-rate exposure, variable-interest-rate products might be the best way to go.

Lines of credit

A line of credit (LOC) is like a mortgage and transaction account combined, similar to a credit card. A LOC has a credit limit, and you can withdraw from and deposit into the LOC as if it were a transaction account (using EFTPOS and ATMs), as long as the balance is always less than this credit limit. Interest is debited from the LOC each month based on the daily balance.

LOCs attract higher interest rates, often in the range of 0.70 per cent to 1.70 per cent per annum higher than package rates.

Unlike the other products we've looked at thus far, LOCs are 'evergreen', which means they don't have a loan term. As such, borrowers are not required to make principal repayments. This can be good and bad. They're not appropriate products for people without a high level of financial discipline.

A LOC might suit an investor who needs to undertake regular small transactions, however, such as someone who's renovating a property. Then, every time you go to the hardware store, for example, you can pay for items electronically, directly from your loan account, making it easy to keep track of your expenses. In my experience, however, apart from in this situation, a LOC is rarely the most suitable product.

Offset accounts

Offset accounts are essentially standard transaction accounts that are linked to your loan account. You can deposit and withdraw funds as usual: the benefit is that the balance in your offset account offsets the balance of the linked loan account.

How this works is that interest is calculated on the net balance of the loan account and the transaction account. For example, if your loan balance was $100,000 and your transaction account balance was $10,000, then you'd be charged loan interest on a net balance of $90,000. The lender performs this calculation at the end of every day, as the amount fluctuates in the offset account, but charges the loan interest monthly.

Any money in the offset account does not earn interest, but will reduce the interest you pay on your mortgage. From a taxation perspective, you're far better off reducing any non-tax-deductible interest (such as the interest on your home loan) than earning interest and paying tax on it. Offset accounts are thus most useful for owner-occupier loans, since you should seek to offset non-tax-deductible debt first before offsetting tax-deductible debt like investment loans.

To maximise the benefit of an offset account, you should direct as much cash flow as possible through it and keep money in the account for as long as possible. For instance, you could have your salary and any rental income deposited into the offset account and pay for as many expenses as possible using a credit card with an interest-free period. This keeps the balance of the offset account high until you pay the credit card balance in full on the due date, avoiding interest charges on your purchases.

The diagram below illustrates this structure. Bear in mind that the name on the loan and the name on the offset account must match each other. See chapter 7 for more on tax.

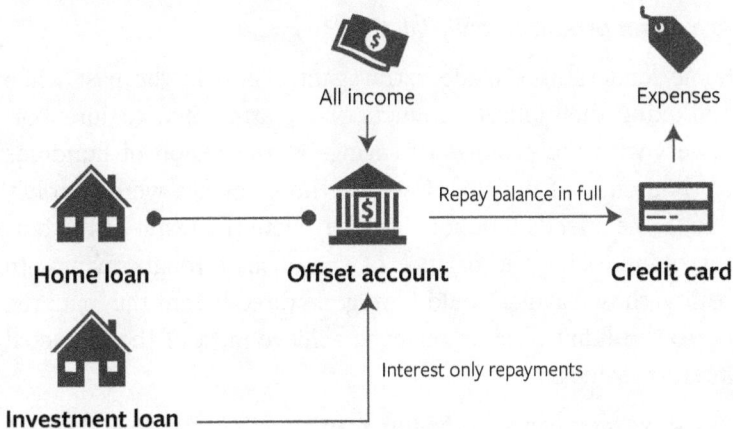

All income

Expenses

Repay balance in full

Home loan   **Offset account**   **Credit card**

Interest only repayments

Investment loan

Generally, lenders will not offer an offset account with a fixed-rate loan: they're only attached to variable-rate products. There are a couple of lenders in Australia that make an exception to this rule, however, which can be very valuable, as they provide you with the double bonus of interest-rate protection and unrestricted 'extra repayments' on your loan. That is, if you have an offset account attached to a fixed-rate loan, you can deposit as much money as you want into that offset, thereby saving yourself interest without triggering any of the penalties that normally apply to extra repayments for fixed-rate loans.

One trick, when a lender allows an offset against a fixed rate, is to apply for two loans. Say you have a home loan of $300,000. What you do is establish two $300,000 loans, one fixed and one variable – both with an offset account attached. Then you can move the surplus $300,000 between the offset accounts depending which rate is higher. This is hedging your bets, as you can offset whichever rate is higher – fixed or variable.

> *An informed borrower is simply less vulnerable to fraud and abuse.* —Alan Greenspan

Are offset products really 'all that'?

Some lenders have made extravagant claims in the past when marketing their offset products. They attempted to lure borrowers with the promise of savings in the region of hundreds of thousands of dollars. However, those savings weren't solely due to the offset's functionality, they were the result of the borrower increasing the balance of the offset through savings. In reality, those savings could have gone directly into the loan: the borrower didn't need an offset to achieve most of the projected interest savings.

Based on my financial modelling, an offset account could save a typical borrower between zero and 5 per cent of the interest cost over the life of the loan. Offset accounts can be very useful for investors – I discuss this in detail in chapter 7.

Offset accounts and repayment frequency

Many people with mortgage commitments are advised to repay their loans fortnightly rather than monthly, for two reasons:

1. The more often you make repayments, the more often the loan principal reduces and therefore the more your interest reduces.
2. Some lenders simply divide the monthly repayment in two to calculate the fortnightly repayment, and this means that borrowers are making 26 'half-monthly' payments per year – essentially, 13 months of repayments.

However, if all your income is paid into your offset account, that first benefit is negated. When you get paid, it's almost as if you've made a notional extra repayment, because your income is offsetting your loan balance. The frequency of your repayments is not such an issue.

Having said that, you may still be able to derive the second benefit of two extra repayments per year by going fortnightly rather than monthly, so it's still wise to choose this option if you have an offset account.

How is an offset different to a line of credit?

I'd suggest an offset account has real benefits compared to a line of credit (LOC). Many mortgage-reduction programs talk about using a LOC to repay your mortgage quicker, but one of the downsides to this approach is that your LOC facility is an all-in-one account. This means that all your money goes into the one account and reduces your loan balance: but this can cause confusion as to what portion is your monthly income and what portion is last month's savings. As a result, borrowers can end up accidentally spending the extra repayment they worked so hard to accumulate.

An offset account will save you just as much as a LOC, but makes it a lot simpler to manage your finances. As soon as your salary hits your account, you know exactly how much you have available and can do what you want with it. If it gets to the end of the month and you have a bit of a surplus left over, you can sweep that money into the loan to reduce the balance. That way, it's out of sight and out of mind. Your salary is deposited again the following month and it's easy to track what you've spent for the month and what you have left over.

Again, there's a psychological barrier associated with redrawing funds from your offset account to fritter away on a frivolous night out, because it's not ultimately benefiting your home loan, whereas it's easier to take money from the ATM with a LOC and give it very little thought. In this way, offsets can maximise your savings and help you manage your money a little bit better than you can with a LOC – the innate flexibility of which often entices people to spend more. So, I'd recommend an offset account over an all-in-one line of credit for most borrowers.

PLAYING TO WIN

Open an offset account attached to non-tax-deductible debt (such as a home loan), wherever economical.

Negotiating interest-rate discounts

Lenders typically offer better deals and discounts to attract new borrowers than they offer to existing customers. So, if you don't regularly check your interest rate and renegotiate it with your lender, then it's likely you're paying more than you need to.

I know that in my business, we contact our clients' existing lenders and proactively negotiate better interest-rate discounts. When was the last time someone from a bank called you up and offered to reduce your interest rate? Never, right? And it's probably never going to happen. So, you have three choices. Firstly, you could build a relationship with a proactive mortgage broker and leave this to them. Secondly, you could contact the bank yourself. Or thirdly, you could do nothing and probably waste thousands of dollars on interest!

If you want to try to negotiate a better discount, you first need to do some research and find a better deal from a comparable lender. There's no point calling up the Commonwealth Bank (CBA) and asking them to match a rate from a lender that's little known, operates completely online and doesn't offer the same products. In that situation, CBA is likely to say that you aren't comparing apples with apples. So, do some research online or call up a mortgage broker and tell them you're looking for information only.

Once you're armed with this data, call your bank and tell them that you're about to sign a discharge authority because you're refinancing to a new lender, but you thought it might be wise to speak to the retention team first, in case they can offer you something to retain your business. Once you get onto the right person, share the details of the competitor offer and it's likely they will offer you high discounts.

Many banks have online chat functions and this can be a quicker, less intrusive way of communicating with them.

How do I choose the best product for me?

There's no denying that not all loan products are created equal. Depending on your personal and financial circumstances, your long-term lending requirements and your goals regarding property investment, certain packages will be a better fit for you than others. So exactly how do you 'try them on for size' and work out the best option? Here are some tips for choosing the right loan product for you.

Get real

Be realistic about the loan features you require: the more features a product has, typically, the higher the cost. Separate your must-have features from the 'nice-to-have'. Redraw is a good example. Often people ask for an investment loan with free (or cheap) redraw, yet in reality, very few investors make extra repayments on an interest-only investment loan. (Remember, borrowers can only redraw 'extra' repayments.) If they do make the odd extra repayment, how likely is it that they'll want to redraw it? Not that likely is my guess. My tip is – focus on the features that matter. (Also, please read chapter 7 for warnings against using redraw with investment loans.)

Consider the loan term

Consider how long you'll hold the property and the loan. If you're going to sell the property in a few years, think about using a discount variable loan to make the most of lower 'honeymoon' rates. If you plan to hold the property for the long term, however, choose the loan that will be the cheapest for, say, the next five years. A five-year period is probably best, as a lot can change in that time in your personal circumstances and in the mortgage market.

Factor in break costs

Break (or early repayment) fees can be an ugly accompaniment to fixed rates, as mentioned earlier. If you plan to sell a property, accumulate material savings, revalue the property to access equity or so forth, then avoiding a fixed-rate product might be the best way to go.

Look for flexibility

Most investors buy and hold property for the long term. However, your needs, perspectives, plans, goals and general approach to your portfolio can change over time. So, it's important to make sure that you maintain your flexibility. Choose a product that will allow you to change the loan without any significant costs. This is one aspect, when it comes to choosing the right mortgage products, that I can't stress enough!

PLAYING TO WIN

Make sure you choose the right product, and don't be confused by the options. Often, you'll only need one of these three types: 1) a package containing a standard variable loan with an interest-rate discount and an offset account, 2) a basic variable-rate loan without an offset or 3) a fixed-rate product.

How do you choose your lender?

Most borrowers skip the first crucial step of finding the right loan product and jump straight to the second question: which is the best lender for me? In reality, you should be asking, 'Which structure is the best for my situation?' (see chapter 6 for more on this) and then 'What products do I need to achieve this structure?' Once you have a clear idea of what you need, you can consider which lender can provide the structure and product you want at the lowest overall cost.

If you're struggling to answer that first question because you just can't get your head around all the marketing hype about loan products, seek advice from a professional who can cut through the hard sell and tell it like it is. In chapter 12, I discuss how to develop a financial strategy and the benefit of getting advice from a mortgage broker.

Interest-only versus principal and interest loans

Interest-only loans and principal and interest (P&I) loans aren't separate mortgage products: they're repayment options that most products provide. Once you've identified the best product for your circumstances, you can consider whether to set up the repayments as interest-only or principal and interest.

The choice between the two options is a conundrum for many investors. Generally, this is because they're flying blind, without the right advice or knowledge of these products and what they offer. So, what's the best way to go?

Although there's a common misconception out there that with an interest-only loan you're limited to paying off solely the interest, the truth is that most variable interest-only products allow you to make unlimited extra repayments. Therefore, you can elect the interest-only option and then repay both principal and interest if you so choose. This provides the best of both worlds: the option to repay either only interest or both principal and interest.

Let's look at an example. On a $100,000 loan with a variable rate of 5 per cent, the interest-only repayments would be $417 per month and the principal and interest repayments would be $537 per month (over a 30-year term). A borrower could set their loan up as interest-only, yet make monthly repayments of $537. At any time, they have the option of reducing their repayments to the base interest-only level (i.e. $417 per month or less, depending on the loan's balance), which provides a very beneficial flexibility. Any principal repayments made during an interest-only term are classified as extra repayments and, as such, they can be redrawn at any time.

Be careful, though. Some lenders don't allow redraw during an interest-only term, so be sure to check this. Also, there can be tax consequences associated with redrawing that you must take into account (see chapter 7 for further details).

Another point to consider is that since the government demanded that Australian banks reduce the volume of new interest-only loans, most lenders have charged higher interest rates for these loans. At the time of writing (December 2019), the average interest-only rate was 0.29 per cent more than the rate for P&I investment loans and 0.57 per cent for P&I owner-occupier home loans. I predict that interest rates for interest-only investment will become more in line with those for P&I loans over the coming years, but that remains to be seen.

After tax, however, the cost of the interest-only premium is between 0.16 per cent and 0.18 per cent (depending on your tax bracket), which isn't a big price to pay for the flexibility that interest-only repayments provide – especially if you share my view that this premium will likely contract or disappear over time. So, is it worth paying the (currently) higher rate for interest-only repayments? The answer to this question depends on your situation, including how close you are to achieving your goals (retirement or financial independence, for example), your level of borrowing and your cash flow. Typically, I would not recommend making principal and interest repayments on investment loans unless you were absolutely certain that you don't plan or need to borrow any more money in your lifetime (e.g. you're retired) or if your cash flow was very strong. If you'd like to learn more about this, I suggest reading my book *Investopoly*, which explains how to develop a financial strategy for yourself using property, shares and super.

Principal and interest products are particularly beneficial for some people. Some borrowers enjoy being 'locked in' to repaying the principal on their loan, so that they're forced to repay their debt over time and don't have to potentially play catch-up down the line.

Ultimately, how you decide to set up your loan is entirely up to you and depends on what you feel most comfortable with. Before you settle on a course of action, though, explore all of your options and ensure that you're making an educated decision.

When the interest-only term expires

Interest-only terms typically only last for between five and ten years. At the end of the term, generally, the loan repayments automatically convert to principal and interest repayments.

At this point, you usually have three options:

1. **Roll over to another interest-only term.** You can ask your bank to roll your loan over to another interest-only term. This is generally possible if your loan was established less than ten years ago.

2. **Refinance your loan with a new lender.** If your current lender isn't willing to offer another interest-only term, you could refinance your loan with another lender. Of course, you'll have to go through an application process, which is quite arduous and time-consuming these days.

3. **Start repaying principal and interest.** The third option is to do nothing and let the loan's repayments convert to principal and interest. One of the advantages of the current low-interest-rate environment is that principal and interest repayments are relatively low.

Loans for building or developing

If you're building or developing a property rather than buying an established property, there are a few differences in loan products to be aware of. Whether you're building your ideal family home or developing properties for investment purposes, you simply won't be able to walk into a bank and get a run-of-the-mill mortgage. This is because building a home takes time and a different financial approach. Let's look at the two types of financing you're likely to encounter if you decide to start from scratch with your own home or to build a development property portfolio: construction loans and development financing.

Construction loans

Essentially, the difference between a construction loan and 'run-of-the-mill' loan is the way the loan amount is provided. When you buy an established property, your lender will simply draw your loan and pay these funds in one lump to the vendor at settlement. When you build a property, however, the funds are provided by the lender directly to the builder in line with the schedule that you have agreed with them.

There are two situations in which construction loans apply, with some variation according to which type of build you undertake: a fixed-price building contract arrangement, or an owner-builder arrangement.

Fixed-price construction loans

A fixed-price building contract is a common and fairly straightforward arrangement put in place when you engage a registered builder to build you a house to agreed specifications and at a fixed price.

With a 'fixed-price' construction loan, payments are made incrementally through a series of what are known as 'progressive drawdowns'. In other words, the lender will pay your builder in stages as dictated in the building contract. Generally, there will be five payments:

1. an initial 10 per cent deposit

2. a second instalment when the slab is poured
3. a third instalment at frame stage
4. a fourth payment when the building reaches lock-up stage
5. a final payment on completion.

These staged payments are written into the contract you receive from the builder when you undertake a fixed-price build. Lenders do this because they're providing funds against the improved value of the property, rather than its initial worth.

So, in a situation where someone buys land for $100,000 and then spends another $100,000 to construct a house on that land, typically the lender will assume that the end value of the property will be $200,000. They will, however, obtain a valuation based on the building specifications and quotes you've received in the fixed-price contract to confirm this assumption.

If they're providing the borrower with 80 per cent of that end value, or $160,000, they will happily lend them $80,000 up-front to settle on the land. When it comes to providing the remaining $80,000 for construction costs, though, they want to ensure that the borrower contributes their money first, and then they pay the builder directly for completed work.

Owner-builder loans

The other situation where construction loans supply funding is with 'owner-builder' arrangements. An owner-builder situation is vastly different and much more complex in many respects than a fixed-price construction loan. The owner of a property, who can either be a registered builder or an 'everyday Joe', undertakes to build their own home and subcontracts the construction work out to different tradespeople.

Not many lenders feel comfortable catering to owner-builders, and of the handful of lenders who will, many offer a significantly lower loan-to-valuation ratio – in the vicinity of 70 per cent or less. A couple of lenders might consider bumping that up to 80 per cent, but mortgage insurers will not touch these types of loans, so this is the absolute maximum you can obtain as an owner-builder.

The reason lenders are reluctant to assist owner-builders is that they present a lot more risk and administrative work – cost blowouts often occur when a layperson chooses to manage their own build without any prior building experience or knowledge. In addition, owner-builders must obtain a builder's licence and conform with other industry requirements, so there's quite a lot of regulatory red tape.

Instead of the loan funds being paid according to a progressive payment schedule, owner-builders have to submit invoices detailing the payments they've made. For example, you would present the bank with your concreter's invoice for $20,000 to show you've paid out that amount for the slab to be poured. The lender would then send someone to visit the site to make sure that the slab has indeed been completed, before reimbursing you the $20,000 from your loan. It can be a time-consuming process, as you're at the mercy of the lender's schedule when it comes to these inspections.

Owner-building is nothing like signing a fixed-price building contract with a professional, where the lender can clearly see all costs involved. In reality, most owner-builders underestimate their costs at the outset and end up knocking on the bank's door for more money halfway through. This places the bank in a catch 22 situation. They don't want a security (i.e. the property) to remain only half-finished and not worth very much, and they're therefore compelled to ensure the client has enough funds to complete the project. That way, they have a property to sell and can recoup any losses should a default situation occur.

* * *

Practically speaking, one of the biggest issues with any type of construction loan is that they're very intensive in terms of administration. When the loan is set up, the borrower normally receives a big pile of documentation to fill out for each progressive payment. If they're using a fixed-cost builder, they have to authorise their lender to release the payments to the builder – as the lender must ensure that the client is happy with the builder's work before they pay for it. The client therefore retains complete control over when the builder is being paid.

However, many banks are quite poor administrators of construction loans, and delays in progressive payments due to red tape can impact negatively on your relationship with the builder. This is one thing to really consider when looking for a lender to finance a construction loan. How good will they be at administration? You might like to talk to their previous customers, or even to a mortgage broker, to gauge which lenders are better when it comes to these specific products.

Generally, lenders will charge a progressive drawdown fee for construction loans, which might be a one-off cost of between $200 and $400 or a per-payment fee of normally around $60 to $100.

Some lenders will do a valuation before the first and last payment – once the slab is down and then again when the Certificate of Occupancy (or similar) has been issued – to make sure the finished product is delivered as promised in the contract. Very few will conduct valuations or inspections at every stage, unless you're owner-building.

Normally, the interest rates for construction loans are the same as for standard loans; however, most construction loans are set up as interest-only until the last progressive payment is made. At this time, it can revert to a principal and interest loan or remain interest-only. The reason that construction loans are set up like this (particularly for fixed-price new-home buyers) is that borrowers are generally renting alternative premises while their home is being constructed, and would struggle to make full repayments on a mortgage for a home that doesn't exist yet.

Also, because the money is drawn down progressively and repayments on principal and interest loans are fixed in terms of dollar value, you don't want to be in a situation where you have a $200,000 construction loan and you've only drawn $20,000, but you're still required to make repayments on the entire loan amount. Once the build is complete and inspections carried out, the lender finalises the loan and switches it over to a normal loan product.

Development finance

A normal residential construction loan is generally used for a development of anything up to and including three dwellings. When you start talking about building more than three properties on an allotment, you enter the domain of development finance. If you're heading in this direction, my advice is to speak with a commercial finance mortgage broker, as it's a specialist field and there are a number of smaller lenders that might offer better financing terms.

PLAYING TO WIN

Many borrowers are bamboozled by all the loan options and risk ending up with the wrong type of product. Typically, there are only five questions you need to focus on:

1. What's the current interest rate?
2. What are the up-front and ongoing fees?
3. Are there any break fees if I switch products or lenders?
4. Can I attach an offset account?
5. Can I make extra repayments?

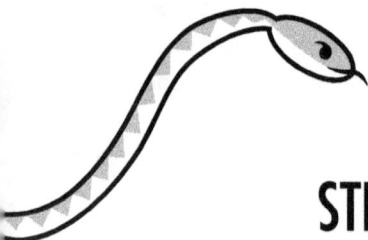

5.
STRUCTURING YOUR LOAN PORTFOLIO

Now that you're familiar with the lending products out there in the marketplace, let's look at the way you structure your investments. As I told you in the previous chapter, it's important to first determine the best structure, then choose the best loan products to build out that structure, and then finally select the best lender to meet your requirements.

Portfolio planning and preparation are crucial to the long-term success of your property investment endeavours, and they go hand-in-hand with structuring. There are two parts to this:

1. the financial structure of your investment property portfolio
2. the ownership structure(s) to hold your properties.

This chapter concentrates on structuring your loan portfolio (the first item), while chapter 6 covers the ownership structures investors can use.

Ironically, while they're trying to save a buck on their next property deal, many investors overlook the importance of how they structure mortgages. They only realise that this area requires at least as much consideration when it's too late and they've lost a pretty penny or reduced their ability to finance more investments.

This may be because many investors lack knowledge when they're starting out, or maybe they're not receiving the best advice. As an investor, however, you need to not only consider what's best for you now, but also think about how your financial decisions will impact on you in the future. Put simply, you need to have a clear and concise plan of attack in all aspects of your property investing, and how you structure your loans is an important part of that plan. Get it right and it could save you thousands. That's exactly what I intend to help you do in this chapter.

PLAYING TO WIN

Understand that selecting the right loan is not just about finding the loan with the lowest interest rate. There are many other important considerations, including tax-effectiveness, cash flow, the ability to make additional investments, risk, flexibility and so on. The interest rate is only one factor – your goal is to optimise the overall wealth-effect of all the considerations.

Why is loan structuring so important?

Loan structure influences many things, including the interest rate and fees you pay, the amount of tax you pay, the amount of flexibility you have, your access to additional finance (i.e. your ability to invest more) and so on. A sound structure will ensure that:

- your debt is tax-effective

- you're able to successfully borrow the amount you need (to invest)
- you aren't tied to or controlled by any lenders
- your risk is contained
- account-keeping is straightforward.

Let's look at these in more detail now.

Ensuring that your debt is tax-effective

A good loan structure will ensure that your debt is tax-effective. One of the most common problems that investors face is an inefficient split of tax-deductible and non-deductible debt. A home loan is a non-tax-deductible debt and an investment loan is a tax-deductible debt. This means simply that the costs associated with setting up and servicing the loan for an investment property can be offset against your assessable income for tax purposes, whereas charges associated with your home loan cannot. It makes sense, then, to have the larger loans (that cost you more) as tax-deductible debt. One of the mistakes many investors make is having their home loan as too large a proportion of their total debt.

Of course, you can't be too tax-focused when it comes to loan structuring, as tax is only one of many considerations. However, optimising your tax position will increase your cash flow – and cash flow is very important when it comes to building an investment-property portfolio.

Retaining your flexibility

By 'flexibility', I mean your ability to make changes to make the most of any opportunities that arise. For example, a flexible structure will allow you to access a sum of money quickly to take advantage of an unexpected investment opportunity, or refinance one of your loans with a lender that's offering a sensational fixed rate for a limited time. An inflexible debt structure, on the other hand, may prevent you from taking the most tax-effective approach.

Containing your risk

Rarely do I meet a prospective client who takes a balanced approach to assessing risk. Investors tend to be either overly conservative, spending too much time focusing on why they shouldn't invest, or blind to risk and looking at everything through rose-coloured glasses. Part of risk management is playing the devil's advocate and thinking about all the things that could go wrong. What if you lose your job? What if you fall ill and can't work? What if a tenant gets injured in your property and sues you?

How you structure your loans can minimise this risk. For example, if you run into financial difficultly, you may decide to sell one of your investment properties and use the cash to pay for living expenses over the next few years. If you have the correct structure in place, this can be a good strategy. However, if your loans are structured incorrectly (e.g. cross-securitised – more on this later) then the bank can control all the sale proceeds and force you to repay debt rather than access the funds to stay afloat.

Improving your account-keeping

The more straightforward your account-keeping is, the happier your accountant and the Australian Taxation Office (ATO) will be. The onus is on the taxpayer to prove why they're claiming certain deductions. For example, if you have one big loan for multiple properties and you sell a property but don't repay any debt (because you believe no debt relates to that property), the onus is on you to demonstrate to the ATO that you're correct. If there's any ambiguity due to poor record keeping, you risk the deduction for interest being denied. A correct loan structure will ensure that you have a sound basis for claiming deductions, as your loans will be separated by property and purpose.

Setting up standalone loans

There are two principal ways to structure your loans – some might say, a right way and a wrong way! In my opinion, in the majority of cases, the right way to structure your investments is to take out standalone loans. The alternative (wrong) way is to cross-securitise – this is covered later in the chapter.

Standalone loans provide the greatest flexibility both immediately and in the future. The general method is to establish a standalone loan – secured by one existing property only – to finance a 20 per cent deposit plus costs and to arrange a further separate loan (secured by the new property only) for the remaining 80 per cent.

Example

An investor has a mortgage of $350,000 on her home, which is valued at $900,000. She wants to purchase an investment property for $600,000. She establishes two separate loans, rather than a single loan for $635,000 (being the purchase price plus costs).

The first loan is for a total of $155,000 (20 per cent deposit plus $35,000 for costs such as stamp duty), which is secured by her existing home. The second loan is for the remaining $480,000 (being the remaining 80 per cent of the purchase price), and is secured only by the investment property. The loan structure looks something like this:

- home loan for $350,000 secured by the investor's home only
- investment loan for $155,000 secured by the investor's home only
- investment loan for $480,000 secured by the new investment property only.

This structure can be employed by investors who only plan to purchase one investment property as well as those who have bigger fish to fry and intend to purchase multiple investment properties.

Flexibility

Many people fail to make any contingency plans for unexpected changes in their circumstances. They might set up a loan structure that's totally suitable for their circumstances today, but that may not offer enough flexibility to adapt to the new state of play tomorrow brings. Remember, life changes are often unexpected and unpredictable, and they're also often unavoidable. How did John Lennon put it? 'Life is what happens to you while you're busy making other plans.'

Thoughts like, 'I'm never going to buy another property!' or 'My bank's been fantastic for the last ten years, so I doubt I'll have any problems in the future!' might be true today, yet they can easily prove fallacious tomorrow. (Also, it's more likely the person you've dealt with is fantastic, not the bank.) You really need to seek out the best advice (given in your best interest) and maintain a flexible loan structure right from the very start.

So, let's consider some of the more important aspects to creating the perfect balance between your present needs and those that might crop up in the future, and look at how to structure your finance for success and maximum benefit.

The following real-life example shows how investors can use a standalone structure to start investing in property and then extend it to buy multiple properties.

Example

Karen and Richard own their home in the Melbourne suburb of Malvern. It's worth approximately $1.5 million and they have a home loan of $370,000. They wanted to start building an investment property portfolio, and had set a budget of up to $750,000 for their first acquisition. They want to then buy a second investment property as soon as they feel comfortable – probably within the next two or three years.

We advised Karen and Richard to access the equity in their home to fund a deposit of 20 per cent plus costs, then to obtain a separate loan for the remaining 80 per cent, secured by the investment property itself.

Step 1: Access deposit funds

Karen and Richard needed access to enough funds to pay for a 10 per cent deposit on the day that they purchased their investment property. So, we arranged a facility to fund 20 per cent, plus costs, plus a buffer. Given they want to buy a second investment property relatively quickly, we actually arranged a facility large enough to accommodate two investment property purchases. Their financial adviser and tax agent have recommended that the investment properties be owned 100 per cent by Karen.

Twenty per cent of $750,000 is $150,000. Costs associated with the purchase include stamp duty ($42,000), legal fees (say $2,000), a buyer's agent fee ($20,000) and a buffer (say $10,000) – approximately $74,000 in total. Therefore, a facility for $450,000 ($150k + $74k = $224k × 2 = $448k) was needed for the two loans' deposits and costs. The loan structure looks like this:

	Loan 1	Loan 2
Loan limit	$370,000	$450,000
Loan balance	$370,000	$214,000
Purpose	Home loan	20% deposits + costs
Applicants	Joint	Karen only
Security	Home only	Home only
Lender	Lender A	Lender A
Comment	Offset 1	Offset 2

Offset 1 is linked to the home loan and Karen and Richard's salary is deposited into this account. This offset will be used to pay for living expenses and home loan repayments. Offset 2 will be in Karen's name only and will be linked to the deposit loan. Any unused loan funds will be deposited into this account and rental income and loan repayments should go into and out from this account.

Once these loans have been established, Karen and Richard are ready to buy their first investment property. On the day of purchase, they will draw the 20 per cent deposit plus costs ($214k) from the new $450k loan.

Step 2: Establish an 80 per cent loan

Once they have purchased their first investment property, they can establish a third loan to fund the remaining 80 per cent of the purchase price. Their purchase budget is $750,000, so 80 per cent is $600,000. Their loan structure will look like this after the investment property purchase is completed.

	Loan 1	Loan 2	Loan 3
Loan limit	$370,000	$450,000	$600,000
Loan balance	$370,000	$214,000	$600,000
Purpose	Home loan	20% deposits + costs	80% loan
Applicants	Joint	Karen only	Karen only
Security	Home only	Home only	New investment property
Lender	Lender A	Lender A	Lender B
Comment	Offset 1	Offset 2	No offset

Note that we used a different lender (Lender B) for the 80 per cent loan.

Step 3: Repeat the process

When Karen and Richard are ready, they can buy their second investment property, as they have access to enough borrowings (from the first $450k deposit loan) to fund another 20 per cent deposit on a property costing

$750,000. Ignoring any changes in the home loan balance, their loan structure will look like this after the second investment property acquisition.

	Loan 1	Loan 2	Loan 3	Loan 4
Loan limit	$370,000	$450,000	$600,000	$600,000
Loan balance	$370,000	$428,000	$600,000	$600,000
Purpose	Home loan	20% deposits + costs	80% loan	80% loan
Applicants	Joint	Karen only	Karen only	Karen only
Security	Home only	Home only	New investment #1	New investment #2
Lender	Lender A	Lender A	Lender B	Lender C
Comment	Offset 1	Offset 2	No offset	No offset

You can see that they still have a small buffer of $22,000 in the deposit loan – the difference between the balance and the limit. Having money available in case of emergencies is important for risk management.

Step 4: Tidy up the loan structure

Since Karen and Richard borrowed 100 per cent of the investment property's purchase price plus costs, they initially needed to use the equity in their home. However, a time will come when they accumulate enough equity in the investment properties to secure their own lending. For example, if the investment properties were to increase in value by 7.5 per cent per year, in five years they'd be worth over $1.07 million each. At this time, we could increase the $600,000 loans (i.e. original 80 per cent loans) by $215,000 to $815,000, and use the extra $215,000 to repay the deposit loan. The investment properties would then stand alone, and the home would no longer be needed for security.

The loan structure would look like this:

	Loan 1	Loan 2	Loan 3	Loan 4
Loan limit	$370,000	$450,000	$600,000	$600,000
Loan balance	$370,000	$Nil	$815,000	$815,000
Purpose	Home loan	20% deposits + costs	Total cost of investment #1	Total cost of investment #2
Applicants	Joint	Karen only	Karen only	Karen only
Security	Home only	Home only	New investment #1	New investment #2
Lender	Lender A	Lender A	Lender B	Lender C
Comment	Offset 1	Offset 2	No offset	No offset

The $450,000 deposit loan can be closed and after the home loan is repaid, Karen and Richard will be able to request the unencumbered title to their home (which is a common goal for most people).

In essence, this loan structure uses the equity in Karen and Richard's home for a limited period of time, until the investment properties accumulate sufficient equity to secure the investment loans.

Funding deposits

In the example, Karen and Richard established one deposit loan that was used to purchase two separate investment properties. Ideally, however, I recommend splitting loans by 'property' and 'purpose' so that you can separately identify what debt relates to which assets. You would establish two deposit loans for $225,000 each, secured solely by the home. I only used one loan for Karen and Richard in the interest of simplicity, and because I intended to clean up the loan structure within the medium term.

Splitting out the deposit loan is more important with more complex structures and more investment properties.

Reviewing your position

You'll gain no benefit from offering lenders more security than you absolutely need to. This is why it's important to review your loan-to-valuation ratio (LVR) on a regular basis – ideally, annually – to identify if the bank still requires all the security it holds or not. Consider the following real-life example from one of my clients.

Security	Loans
Home value $1,500,000	Home loan for $270,000
Investment value $500,000	Investment loan for $205,000

Here, the client's lender had the first mortgage over property worth $2 million to secure $475,000 of lending. That equates to an LVR of less than 24 per cent. In this situation, it was completely unnecessary for the client to offer the investment property as security – the home alone would have been more than satisfactory.

The rule of thumb is to aim to maintain an LVR as close to 80 per cent as possible. If the LVR reduces significantly, consider requesting that the lender release a property from security (as we did in the above example). Prudent investors must always protect their assets as much as possible and maintain control.

> *Money is plentiful for those who understand the simple laws which govern its acquisition.* —George Clason

Should you spread your borrowings across multiple lenders?

You'll have noticed that in Karen and Richard's case, we used three different lenders: Lender A, B and C. As an investor, it's often a good idea to use a number of lenders rather than keeping all your eggs in one basket. The concern is that if you have all of your lending with one bank and something goes awry – say, there's a breakdown in your relationship or a disagreement that can't be resolved – you could find yourself at the mercy of a lender who holds sway over all your mortgages. In fact, this is the most valuable lesson the GFC and, more recently, the credit crunch of 2017 and 2018 has taught me. Prior to these events, I was less convinced that using multiple lenders was a real advantage. However, during the GFC and the credit crunch, lenders tightened credit policies for 'new to bank' customers (i.e. people who didn't have existing lending with them) and kept credit policy more relaxed for existing customers. This meant that borrowers using multiple lenders had more borrowing options.

The other advantage of using different lenders is that it allows you to control information flow. For example, if you have all your lending with one provider and you apply for another investment loan, that provider can see all your details – what you spend and earn – via your transaction account. If you separate your transactional banking and lending, you have control over what information the lender has access to. I'm not suggesting that you should purposefully withhold information, just that you should have control over it. This is particularly important for self-employed borrowers, as we'll discuss a little later.

That said, one advantage of having all your lending with one lender is that you may be able to negotiate better interest rates or fees. Also, a lender may be more willing to approve a loan that's 'outside the square' if you have all your lending with them, because they have all your accounts and information and will be one of the first to know if your financial situation deteriorates.

On balance, though, I recommend using different lenders if this doesn't limit your options, increase complexity or give rise to significantly higher costs. Remember, it's not something you can rectify later when you run into trouble – you can't, for example, use one lender with the intention of diversifying if you have problems in the future, as it'll often then be too late to change. Spreading your lending across a few lenders is a prudent risk-management practice, and these days I'm pretty keen to see my clients diversify their borrowing relationships where it's logical and appropriate.

This is even more important when you have business and personal borrowings with the same bank. I normally recommend using separate banking institutions for business lending and personal (and investment) lending. As the saying goes, never mix business with pleasure. I've heard too many horrifying stories about what can happen when you do!

About cross-securitisation

'Cross-securitisation' is where a mortgage is secured by two or more properties. You can have multiple loans secured by one property (that's okay), but not multiple properties securing one loan – that's cross-securitisation and it's bad!

A typical situation is an investment loan that's secured by both an owner-occupied home and investment property, as shown in the illustration overleaf.

This structure may not pose too many problems for investors who own just one investment property, but if you plan to build a portfolio consisting of many properties, it's not optimal, as it reduces flexibility. Making sure you have an optimal structure from the outset will save you hassle and money later on.

In the scenario shown in the diagram, the investor cannot move their investment loan away from this lender, as it represents 109 per cent of the property's value and relies on the home for additional security. So, what would happen if the lender decided to increase interest rates on investment loans? What happens if the bank is more conservative about borrowing capacity than other lenders, and won't lend the investor any more money? The borrower would have to refinance both of their loans with other lenders in order to borrow more. This may not be a huge hassle with two loans, but imagine if you had ten different loans!

**Each loan is secured by both
the home and investment property**

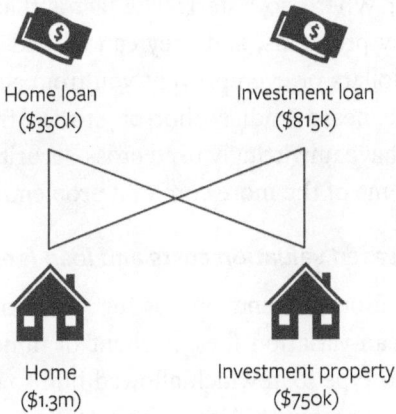

Home loan
($350k)

Investment loan
($815k)

Home
($1.3m)

Investment property
($750k)

Some advisers suggest that cross-securing your property portfolio gives rise to higher risk because if all properties are securing all loans and something goes wrong, the bank can sell the lot. I don't subscribe to this theory. Firstly, most mortgage contracts have 'all monies' clauses which essentially allow the lender to consolidate all loans associated with one borrower, regardless of how they're structured. Also, from a practical perspective, if you get into financial strife, it's unlikely you'll only default on one mortgage and keep the repayments up on the rest. More likely than not, you won't be able to meet any repayments. So, I don't believe that avoiding cross-securitisation will help you a lot.

Cross-securitisation is often described as 'insidious', which according to Merriam-Webster's dictionary means 'developing so gradually as to be well established before becoming apparent'. In other words, the detrimental effects of cross-securitisation are often not obvious until it's too late. This is why it can be difficult to impress on new investors the importance of structuring their loans correctly from the beginning. However, if you speak to investors who have been bitten by cross-securitisation, they appreciate all too well the importance of a correct loan structure.

So, what are the real concerns when it comes to cross-securitising property loans? Where do I start? The fact is that this approach can cause many problems, and they can all end up costing you thousands of dollars or even prevent you from acquiring further properties. I've heard endless horror stories from misguided investors who have unwittingly used cross-securitisation. Let me fill you in on some of the more common problems.

There are increased valuation costs and loan fees

Cross-securitisation can end up costing you more in valuation and possibly loan-variation fees. A client of mine, for example, used a portfolio-type loan which allowed him to easily establish separate sub-loan accounts. Although portfolio loan products are very flexible, in my opinion they're rarely appropriate, as they're inherently cross-securitised – all property is pooled together as security for all associated loan accounts and limits. This particular client owned two investment properties plus his own home, and wanted to increase one of his sub-loan accounts by a small amount to dabble in some share investing. In order to do this, the bank had to order valuations on all three properties, because they were cross-securitised. This ended up costing him quite a lot of money for a very small loan increase. If he'd have had all the loans individually secured, he would have had the flexibility to choose which property he wanted revalued, and saved himself over $500 in the process.

Flexibility is reduced

If your loans are cross-secured, you may not be able to choose the best current deal going in the market. Consider the earlier example in which the investor had a home loan for $350,000 and an investment loan for $815,000. Assume this investor wants to fix his investment loan for three years because several lenders are offering some very attractive fixed rates. Since his loans are cross-secured, he is limited to three options:

1. He can accept the fixed rate that his existing lender is offering, even though other lenders are offering lower rates.
2. He can refinance all his lending with a new lender that offers the lowest fixed rates, and deal with the hassle that a refinance can create, including moving transactional banking.
3. He can restructure his existing lending to uncross-securitise his loans and refinance a portion of his investment loan with a new lender – again, this is a lot of hassle.

None of these three options is optimal, as each is likely to trigger unnecessary costs, consume a lot of time or force the investor to settle for a fixed rate that's not the most competitive. If the investor's loans were standalone, it would make life a lot easier. He'd simply have to refinance the standalone investment loan with a lender that offered the lowest-cost fixed rate; he wouldn't need to alter his home loan at all, avoiding the extra cost of doing this.

There's limited scope for negotiation

Cross-securitisation reduces your negotiating power, particularly with your existing lender. If you're negotiating with this lender for, say, a fixed rate, they will normally consider the consequences of not matching the best rate on the market. If your loans are poorly structured, the lender knows that you'll probably have to refinance all your lending elsewhere to get the lowest fixed rate. They might assume that you're unlikely to be bothered going to this trouble – and therefore, they won't be as willing to match the lowest fixed rate, figuring they'll retain your business anyway. If your loans are standalone and you can easily refinance one away from your existing lender, they'll feel that all your business is 'at risk' and will be more likely to match the best fixed rate going.

Banks rarely have much loyalty to their customers and will generally only discount their rates as a last resort – I've never heard of a lender offering a customer a discount just because they've been loyal! They need to fear that they'll lose your business first. So, a flexible loan structure shifts some of the negotiating power back to you, because you're not handcuffed to the bank and at their mercy.

It's expensive to break from fixed-interest set-ups

It's particularly important to avoid cross-securitisation if fixed-interest rate loans are involved, as it can be very costly to change this type of loan during the fixed term. As discussed in chapter 4, most lenders will charge break fees ranging from a negligible amount to thousands of dollars (with the amount of the fee depending on the fixed rates at the time).

Let's take that previous example again, but assume that when the investment loan for $815,000 was established, it was fixed for three years at 5 per cent. One year on and fixed rates have decreased, with the current two-year and three-year fixed rates at approximately 4 per cent. The investor has plenty of equity in his home and decides it's the right time to purchase another investment property. He initially approaches his existing lender, but they have, frustratingly, become ultraconservative and have significantly curtailed their lending policies. They decline to lend him any more money due to serviceability issues. However, more than ten other lenders will happily lend him enough capital to purchase another investment property. Now, the investor has two choices. He can:

1. refinance his existing loans with one of the ten lenders, thereby breaking his existing fixed-rate loan and paying approximately $20,000 in fees due to the rate decrease

2. wait to purchase another investment property until the fixed-rate loan expires in two years, and refinance then (and property prices may have risen by that time).

Once again, these two options are quite inadequate and either will cost our hapless investor thousands of dollars. If the loans were not cross-secured, he could have left the fixed-rate loan with his existing lender and simply refinanced the home-loan portion to a new lender, then accessed some of the equity in his home for the second investment purchase.

It hampers your borrowing capacity

Investors can extend their borrowing capacity by using particular lenders, but this is only possible with careful planning when setting up the loan structure. The strategy is to use lenders with the lower borrowing capacities for your deposit-and-costs loans first, and arrange access to equity in existing properties. You can then use lenders with higher borrowing capacities to borrow the remaining 80 per cent of your investment loans. (Higher borrowing capacities are often due to the fact that some lenders don't add an interest-rate margin onto any existing mortgage repayments you have with other lenders.) This strategy isn't feasible unless you avoid cross-securitisation.

It provides lenders with too much security

As we saw in the earlier section, 'Reviewing your position', you don't want to give lenders more security in your property than necessary. Cross-securitisation can result in you providing a lender with too much security, and potentially handing your own home and your investment property to the bank on a platter. In my experience, cross-securitisation is often not necessary: often, the investor's home provides satisfactory security by itself, if they have enough equity in it.

It's important to note that the security offered does not affect the tax-effectiveness of the loan – an investment loan secured by your home can still be tax-deductible.

Many investors end up giving their bank a mortgage over the new investment property when it's not necessary, and when, in reality, they could have held the title to this property without any encumbrances.

Risk of lower valuation and reduced available equity

If your loans are cross-secured, the bank will revalue all your properties at the same time, and the risk is that lower valuations could offset higher ones, thereby reducing your 'available' equity. Having loans individually secured, by contrast, allows you to cherrypick which properties to revalue.

Loss of control

Assume that you have multiple properties that are all cross-secured with the same lender. If you sell one of your properties, the lender has to consent to releasing the title, and may only agree to do so on the condition that you use all of the sale proceeds to reduce your other debt (i.e. to reduce your total debt exposure). In other words, the lender may control how you use your money in this situation. If the loan is standalone, however, then you only have to repay the loan that's directly secured by the property you sell, and can retain whatever money is left.

* * *

These are just a few of the reasons it pays to tread carefully when structuring your loans and make sure that they'll serve you best in the long run. There are many more ways that cross-securitisation can negatively affect you; I come across new examples regularly.

So, is cross-securitisation all bad?

Is cross-securitisation all bad? Perhaps the question should be, are there any situations in which cross-securitisation is good? I'd suggest that there are limited situations in which cross-securitisation is beneficial.

It's probably not very detrimental for investors who only ever purchase one investment property and won't need to alter their lending in the future. I'd still advise such investors to proceed with caution, though, because plans and bank credit polices often change and consequently their lending requirements may change too. Some investors start out thinking that they'll only ever purchase one investment property, but a couple of years and a few bites from the property bug later, they're singing a different tune. So, regardless of what your plans are today, you really should maintain flexibility for tomorrow.

One instance where cross-securitisation might be worthwhile is where an investor has borrowed a significant amount: say, more than $4 or $5 million. Some lenders will insist on cross-securitising loans at this debt level, or will offer an extra interest-rate discount for cross-securitisation. Given the potential interest saving, it might be worthwhile accepting the cross-securitisation in this case, but it very much depends on the lender, the strength of the application and the customer or broker's relationship with that lender.

Some people may feel that another benefit of cross-securitisation is that it can involve less hassle and expense than establishing several separate standalone loan accounts. This may be true, but once the standalone loans are set up correctly, most borrowers get used to the extra complexity, as many of the loan accounts will be 'set and forget'.

PLAYING TO WIN

Do not cross-secure home and investment loans! Cross-securitisation is where a mortgage is secured by two or more properties. The most common structure (mistake) is to have an investment loan secured by both the person's home and the investment property.

The costs of avoiding cross-securitisation

As discussed in chapter 4, many lenders offer packages which bundle up a number of banking products (e.g. home loan, credit card and transaction account) and offer interest-rate discounts. One of the benefits of such packages is that many allow borrowers to set up several (often five but sometimes unlimited) separate mortgage accounts without any extra upfront or ongoing fees. This is excellent from a loan-structuring perspective, as it allows you to set up the perfect structure every time.

However, if you can't benefit from a package for some reason, then you have to weigh up the costs and advantages of using an optimal, standalone structure. Avoiding cross-securitisation may require you to set up two separate loans, for example, and there-fore potentially pay two application fees and two monthly fees. In this situation, I wouldn't always suggest that this is the best way to go. You do need to be mindful of costs and find the right balance between minimising these and creating an optimal loan structure.

Other considerations include practicality, usability and simplicity. If avoiding cross-securitisation means a client needs to establish a large number of accounts and loan facilities, then I may sometimes opt for a more streamlined structure with cross-securitisation. For some people, simplicity is more important.

It's never too late

If you already own a substantial property portfolio and think, after reading this, that you may have made a few blunders when setting up your loan structure – don't panic. There are ways and means of addressing an inadequate loan structure: it's just a bit more of a bumpy road to navigate when you've already progressed part of the way down it.

Perhaps it's best to define here what I mean by a 'bad structure'. In my opinion, a bad structure is one that has cross-securitisation and perhaps a lack of distinction between debts – that is, where it's difficult to identify what debt relates to which property, what's tax-deductible debt and what's not.

While it's not impossible, unwinding a debt structure can be difficult. A bad loan structure (for you) is generally good for the lender, because it provides them with better security and ties you to them. There's little incentive for them to change that structure. Furthermore, in most instances there's no incentive for the staff member you get hold of to provide assistance. Changing the loan structure might take up a lot of their time, as it's essentially a whole new application process, and often staff members are only rewarded for bringing in 'new' debt. As such, they might be reluctant to spend time changing an existing structure, as there's nothing in it for them!

Combine these two factors and you're likely to experience some resistance when you ask to undo the cross-securitisation of your loans. The best way to deal with this issue (if your initial kind requests are ignored) is to threaten to take your business elsewhere. Often, that provides lenders with enough incentive to attend to your requests promptly.

Generally, fixing a bad structure involves changing and/or splitting a few loans. Often, packages (discussed in chapter 4) will allow you to do this at no or very little cost.

Using the earlier example of cross-securitisation, what we'd need to do is split the $815,000 investment loan into two: one loan for $215,000 and one for $600,000. The $600k loan can be secured solely by the investment property, so that the LVR is 80 per cent, which is typically the maximum you can borrow without paying lenders mortgage insurance. The $215k loan can be secured by the home only. Here's how it looks before and after the split:

With cross-securitisation

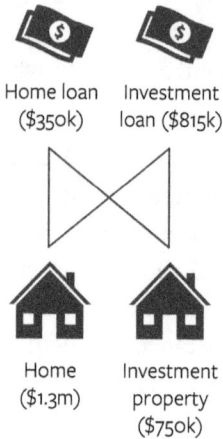

Home loan
($350k)

Investment
loan ($815k)

Home
($1.3m)

Investment
property
($750k)

Without cross-securitisation

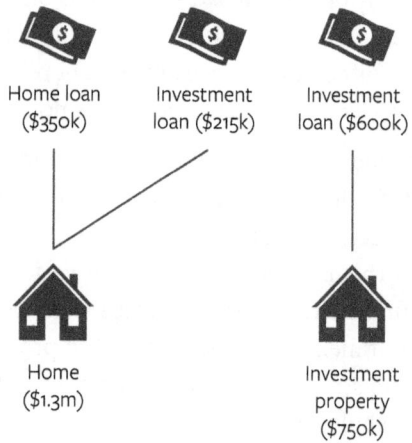

Home loan
($350k)

Investment
loan ($215k)

Investment
loan ($600k)

Home
($1.3m)

Investment
property
($750k)

As I touched upon earlier, if you're locked into a fixed-interest rate period, attempting to wind the clock back and restructure your loans may trigger significant break fees. If this is the case, you might have to be a little bit patient and wait until your fixed rates expire before optimising your structure.

If in doubt, you should always seek advice from a knowledgeable and licensed professional. The benefits of unwinding cross-securitisation are considerable.

Avoiding mortgage-insurance mayhem

Remember the discussion of lenders mortgage insurance (LMI) in chapter 1? Well, LMI is also a consideration when it comes to setting up your loan structure. You already know that LMI can be a substantial purchasing cost, but you may not realise that this cost can be minimised by structuring individual loans effectively. Perhaps the best way to demonstrate this is via an example.

Example

Assume that an investor owns two investment properties and needs to increase her lending by $65,000 to fund a deposit for another property purchase. The property and loan values are shown in the following table.

	Value	Mortgage	LVR
Property 1	$850,000	$715,000	84.1%
Property 2	$650,000	$515,000	79.2%
Total	$1,500,000	$1,230,000	81.7%
Additional funds required		$65,000	
Total lending required		$1,295,000	86.3%

The investor has two options.

Option 1: Increase both individual loans to 86.3 per cent of the properties' values and pay mortgage insurance on both loans (remember, LMI kicks in at above 80 per cent):

Existing loan	New loan amount	LVR	Cost of LMI
$715,000	$734,000	86.4%	$12,200
$515,000	$561,000	86.3%	$9,000
Total increase = $65,000			$21,200

Option 2: Increase one loan to 91.8 per cent and leave the remaining loan unchanged, thereby only paying mortgage insurance on the one loan:

Existing loan	New loan amount	LVR	Cost of LMI
$715,000	$780,000	91.8%	$30,000
$515,000	$515,000	79.2%	Nil
Total increase = $65,000			$30,000

Now, obviously most people would not pay $20,000 to $30,000 in mortgage insurance fees just to access an additional $65,000 of borrowings! But you can see that using standalone loans can help you manage the cost of mortgage insurance, as you can increase or reduce individual loan amounts to minimise the cost of LMI.

It's important to note that the cost of LMI can vary greatly between lenders. For instance, at the time of writing, for the 91.8 per cent LVR in option 2, the cost of LMI ranges between $28,500 and $34,000 depending on the lender – which is a massive difference! One of the benefits of having a flexible loan structure is that you can use any lender you like.

Setting up your loan structure

It's handy to have an appreciation for the steps a lender will take when establishing your optimal loan structure. Loan structures, borrowers' personal circumstances and lenders' policies and processes are all different, so no two applications are the same. However, this is a guide to what to expect after you've completed and signed a loan-application form and provided all your supporting documents, such as pay slips and bank statements:

1. **Verification.** The first step for the bank is to ensure that they have all the relevant information. If there's something unique about your circumstances, they may request additional documents.

2. **Conditional approval.** Your file will then be sent to a credit assessor and they'll complete an assessment. They may have questions or ask for additional documents. If the loan is outside of their delegated approval limit, they may have to refer the file to someone more senior to approve it. If you're borrowing more than 80 per cent of the property's value, the mortgage insurers may also have to approve it. If the bank is comfortable with your application, it will approve it, conditional upon you satisfying additional items. This might include providing additional evidence or documents. However, the most common conditional item is a satisfactory valuation of the property.

3. **Property valuation.** The bank will order a valuation on the property or properties that you're using as security. Normally, valuations are completed within two to three days, subject to the valuer being able to gain access to the property, if required.

4. **Unconditional approval.** Once the valuation has been satisfactorily completed and all other conditional items have been satisfied, the credit department will unconditionally approve your loan and confirm this in writing.

5. **Loan documents.** After a loan is unconditionally approved, the bank will prepare loan documents and send them to you for signing. Many banks do this electronically these days.

6. **Certify ready for settlement.** Once you've signed the loan documents and provided any additional documentation (often proof of building insurance), the bank will check everything to ensure it's been signed correctly. If it has, the loan will be certified as ready to settle.

7. **Settlement.** The bank will book in settlement. If you're purchasing a property, the bank will contact your conveyancer and arrange this. If you're refinancing a loan from another lender, the bank will contact that lender. You don't need to attend settlement – this occurs between the banks themselves.

I cannot stress enough that you should get pre-approvals before you purchase a property. A pre-approval is when a bank has reviewed your loan application and given you approval to borrow a certain amount, at a certain LVR, before you've found a property. This not only saves you (and your broker) time and stress, but it also puts you in a position of strength compared to other potential purchasers, as you can be reasonably sure your finance will be approved. In addition, lenders can normally settle quicker if they've pre-approved your loan, which is a good 'non-cash' bargaining tool.

PLAYING TO WIN

Get your finance pre-approved. It's foolish to think you can sort out your loan approval after you've purchased your property, particularly as credit policies have changed so much in recent years. Murphy's Law suggests that if you leave it to the last minute, you're inviting problems and delays. Obtain a pre-approval; it's less stress for everyone.

FIXED RATES: BE WARNED

At the risk of sounding like a broken record, may I repeat that you need to tread very carefully when using fixed-rate products in a loan structure. The combination of a bad structure and fixed rates can be crippling, as fixed-interest-rate loans have the effect of freezing a structure into place for the term of the fixed rate.

Investors tend to change their loans more often than owner-occupiers, so I would caution using a fixed rate for an investment loan unless you have a very firm reason for doing so. Changes might include increasing your loan, selling the property or switching lenders, and can be motivated simply by a change of investment strategy or an opportunity presenting itself. Less than 10 per cent of mortgages are fixed-rate loans in Australia, and there's a very good reason for that.

If you are going to fix one of your loans, then make sure it's stand-alone, not cross-securitised. That way you minimise the chances of triggering break fees.

It's all about the future

If you think that you'll never want to own more than one or two investment properties, then loan structure is important but maybe not critical. However, if you're a more serious investor and plan to build a significant property portfolio, thinking about your loan structure from the beginning can save you a lot of heartache down the track.

In my experience, loan structuring is overlooked by many investors, mortgage brokers and lenders. As the saying goes, though, 'If you fail to plan then you plan to fail!' It's an important factor that needs to be considered not only in the beginning, but on a regular basis as your property portfolio changes.

To summarise what has been a long chapter, my loan structuring tips are:

- Avoid cross-securitisation.
- Choose interest-only repayments (as discussed in the previous chapter).
- Plan for the future.
- Consider the future use of the property and the effect of repaying debt.

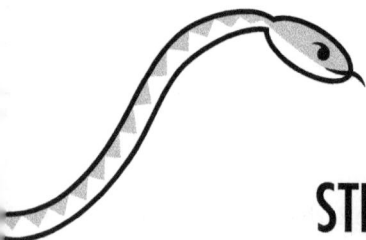

6.

STRUCTURING YOUR LOANS IN A COMPANY OR FAMILY TRUST

Buying and selling real estate isn't just about putting your name on the title and becoming the proud owner of numerous properties. There's more involved, including maximising the taxation, cash flow and legal benefits you derive from your portfolio to ensure that you achieve your long-term goals. To do this, you need to choose the best ownership structure for your investments. So, let's delve into the nitty-gritty of planning and preparing your property portfolio.

The majority of property investors set up their portfolio as a solo investor or jointly with their partner. However, there are many more options to consider when you get into the groove of property investing and start to become a little more savvy about how you structure your property acquisitions.

The legal, financial and taxation aspects of different ways of structuring a portfolio can have all sorts of implications, positive and negative. So, just as it's important to think about loan structure before you set out to make millions from property investing, it's crucial to have a clear direction when you're putting legal structures in place, so that you maximise your capacity to create and retain wealth through property.

Many investors ask me whether they should set up a company or trust to own their prospective property investments. We'll discuss various ownership options now, but please don't go setting up any structures purely based on reading this chapter. Seek advice about ownership options from your accountant (i.e. a registered tax agent who's also experienced with property investment), your financial adviser (if you have one, as there are cash flow and planning implications) and your mortgage broker or banker (as your decision could have loan-structure implications). You need input from all three parties, so you get a holistic picture of the pros and cons of different structures. Alternatively, you could engage a holistic firm that's licensed and experienced enough to address all the relevant considerations.

You must get personalised advice: the information in this book is general in nature. With that caveat, let's look at how trusts could be used in an investment portfolio ownership structure.

Investing through a company

Typically, I would recommend against investing in property via a company, mainly because a company is not entitled to a 50 per cent capital gains tax discount (whereas individuals and trusts are). This means an investor who uses a company will pay a higher rate of capital gains tax. However, in some limited circumstances (particularly for self-employed people), a company may be appropriate. For the sake of simplicity, I will only discuss investing via a trust in this chapter; however, the loan structuring concepts equally apply to companies.

Investing through a trust

The most common trust is a discretionary or 'family' trust. One of the benefits of a discretionary trust is that it provides tax-planning flexibility, in that the trustee can distribute income and capital to beneficiaries with (often) complete discretion. The other main benefit is asset protection – that is, no-one owns a trust's assets until the trustee chooses to distribute them. (The trustee is the person or entity that's responsible for dealing with the assets of the trust in accordance with the rules of the trust – that is, the trust deed). This means that, if you were declared bankrupt, for example, it's likely that a property owned by a family trust would be protected from creditors. This isn't ironclad, but as a general principle, a trust provides a good level of protection.

So, how can you use a trust to buy property? Let's say your accountant has established a new family trust for you and you plan to use it to purchase an investment property. You have equity in your home, which you decide to access to assist with this acquisition. You're aware that you should avoid cross-securitisation, so you've opted to establish a deposit loan (i.e. a loan large enough to fund a 20 per cent deposit plus costs, including stamp duty) secured solely by your home. This loan is taken out by the trust. The remaining 80 per cent will be funded via a separate loan, also taken out in the name of the trust, and using only the trust's property (the new acquisition) as security.

Quite often we see these two loans set up incorrectly, with the first loan (the deposit loan) established in personal names – that is, in the name of the individuals, not the trust. This may have been done because it's easier (since the home is in personal names) or because it costs slightly less (as putting the loan in the trust's name could incur additional bank fees, since different products may apply and the bank will typically have a lawyer review the trust deeds to ensure it has the power to borrow).

The problem with this approach is that it means that you, the borrower, now have a personal asset and liability: the asset is the money that the trust owes you and the liability is the bank loan. A trustee in bankruptcy could thus potentially force you to call in the trust's loan, forcing the trust to repay it. In the event that the trust couldn't repay it – which it probably wouldn't be able to do, because you're in financial difficulty and/or because it may not hold a lot of cash or liquid assets – the trustee would have to sell the property. For this reason, all debt should be in the trust's name. The loan structure for the deposit loan would have the trust as the sole applicant and the individuals as guarantors – the guarantors provide the security for the loan (i.e. the home), and the income.

As you know from chapter 5, I'm nearly always against cross-securitisation – but even more so when an entity such as a trust is involved. It's unlikely that I would agree to having one loan in the trust's name for the entire purchase price plus costs, and secured by both the trust's property and the home (i.e. cross-securitised). It is important that there are two separate loans, one against each security.

Just to clarify one issue, when I say the loan is to be in the trust's name, I actually mean it will be in the trustee's name. The name will be something like, 'Wemyss Investments Pty Ltd as trustee for (ATF) The Wemyss Family Trust'. The trustee has to be named, as it legally holds the property on behalf of the trust.

A simple trust structure

When you invest in property via a trust, the trustee holds the property on behalf of the trust: the property title is registered in the trustee's name. Usually, the trustee is a company (as in the 'Wemyss Investments Pty Ltd' example). The trustee normally borrows the money on behalf of the trust, so the loan will also be in the trustee's name.

In some circumstances, where an investor uses a hybrid discretionary trust (i.e. the investor borrows money to purchase income units in the hybrid discretionary trust), the loan might be in that investor's name. I will discuss this in detail a little later in this chapter.

Perhaps the best way to explain how to structure lending via a trust is through an example.

Example

Rick and Andrea own their home (in joint names). It's worth approximately $1.5 million and they have a home loan for $350,000. They decide that they'd like to purchase an investment property for $800,000 and have been advised to set up a discretionary trust for this purpose.

Step 1: Access deposit funds

The first thing Rick and Andrea need to do is set up a new lending facility so that they can access the equity in their existing home to use as a deposit. They'll need enough money to pay a 20 per cent deposit plus costs (e.g. stamp duty). The costs associated with an $800,000 purchase amount to around $47,000, so they'll need to set up a loan for $210,000 – a 20 per cent deposit of $160,000 plus $47,000 costs, rounded up.

This deposit loan will be in the name of their trustee: let's call it 'R & A Trustee Pty Ltd as trustee for The Rick & Andrea Family Trust'. Their loan structure will look like this:

Loan	Amount	Secured by	Applicant
Home loan	$350,000	Home only	Personal
Investment loan	$210,000	Home only	R & A Trustee Pty Ltd ATF The Rick & Andrea Family Trust

Note that some lenders won't lend to family trusts, or if they do, use a different fee and interest rate structure for such loans. Select your lender very carefully! It's likely that the lender will ask for personal guarantees from all directors of the trustee company, in this case R & A Trustee Pty Ltd.

Step 2: Get pre-approval for the 80 per cent loan

Rick and Andrea will also obtain a pre-approval from a lender for a loan of $640,000 (the remaining 80 per cent of the property's purchase price). This loan will be in the trustee's name; however, since the trust is a newly formed entity and earns no income in its own right, the lender will certainly require a personal guarantee from all directors of the trustee company. The loan structure will be as follows:

Loan	Amount	Secured by	Applicant
Home loan	$350,000	Home only	Personal
Investment loan	$210,000	Home only	R & A Trustee Pty Ltd ATF The Rick & Andrea Family Trust
Pre-approval	$640,000	New property only	R & A Trustee Pty Ltd ATF The Rick & Andrea Family Trust

Step 3: Draw deposit funds and establish the 80 per cent loan

Once they've selected an investment property, Rick and Andrea will pay the 10 per cent deposit from the $210,000 loan facility. On settlement, they'll pay another 10 per cent plus costs, again from this facility. The bank will then set up the new $640,000 loan in the name of the trustee company for the remaining funds.

The key benefit of this structure is that there is no cross-securitisation, which means there is a good separation between the investors' personal assets (i.e. their own home) and their investments. In addition, all LVRs are 80 per cent or less, so lenders mortgage insurance isn't required. In probably five to ten years' time, let's say, the trust's property has increased in value from $800,000 to over $1,063,000. Rick and Andrea can then combine the two trust loans into a single loan solely secured by the trust's property, as the equity in the home is no longer required.

Hybrid and unit trusts

A unit trust is a trust that can issue units to beneficiaries to create a fixed entitlement to the trust's income or capital – much like shares in a company. For example, if you own 30 per cent of a trust's issued units, then you're entitled to 30 per cent of its income and/or capital (depending on the unit type).

A hybrid trust is essentially a discretionary trust that has the power to issue units to create a fixed entitlement.

Only a handful of lenders in Australia will lend to a unit trust, and hybrid trusts are even more unpopular. The reason for this is that unit holders can on-sell their units in the trust to a third party, which might affect the lender's capacity to act upon any guarantees. There are rumours that one bank actually suffered losses because of this very situation. Due to the small number of lenders and many other reasons, I'd caution anyone against using these entities.

Self-managed superannuation funds

A self-managed superannuation fund (SMSF) is also a trust structure. An SMSF is allowed to borrow to buy property, under what are called 'limited recourse borrowing arrangements' (or LRBA).

However, as with unit and hybrid trusts, only a small pool of lenders will lend money to an SMSF – and most of the larger, well-known banks don't offer these loans anymore. In addition, credit parameters have tightened considerably. The Australian Tax Office is also clamping down on a number of compliance issues, and this can affect whether borrowing to buy property via a super fund is an efficient strategy or not.

This is a very complex area and there are a number of tax and financial-planning factors to consider, which are beyond the scope of this book. If you do want to investigate this option, I recommend seeking advice from a holistic firm that is able (licensed and experienced) to help you weigh up the borrowing, financial, retirement and tax considerations.

Don't sign a general security agreement

This may be a thing of the past, as I haven't come across it for a while, but it's still worth mentioning: do not sign a general security agreement (GSA). Sometimes called 'registered mortgage debentures', a GSA is essentially a floating charge over the borrower entity's current and future assets. GSAs are more commonplace in business lending, but a GSA is overkill if the borrower is a non-trading investment entity such as a family trust. The trust already has adequate security in the form of the registered first mortgage over the property. Also, other lenders will be less willing to lend to an entity if there's a GSA with another lender. The simple solution is, don't agree to one.

Personal guarantees

When a loan application is in an entity's name (whether company, trust or super fund) nearly all lenders will insist on all interested (or controlling) parties providing personal guarantees. The main reason for this is that the entity alone often doesn't have sufficient income to service the debt. Also, people controlling the entity could purposely drain it of assets to avoid having to meet the loan repayments. So, the lender wants the controlling parties to take responsibility for the debt.

I've only once obtained approval for a loan to be in a family trust's name without the bank asking for personal guarantees. This occurred pre-GFC – I doubt the same deal would be approved today.

Most banks will seek guarantees from all trustees (if the trustees are individuals) or all directors of a corporate trustee. I've seen some banks ask for guarantees from all beneficiaries as well – anyone who's received a distribution of funds from the trust in the preceding two years – which is a bit ridiculous, given that beneficiaries can change from year to year. I'd advise against agreeing to this.

When setting up your structures, consider who will need to provide a guarantee. It might be better, for example, to only have one person in a married couple as director of the trustee company, so that the other spouse's borrowing capacity is preserved. Longer-term credit planning can be useful in this regard.

Most guarantees are 'joint and several', which means each individual guarantor is responsible for the entire debt. This is an important point to be aware of if you're investing with friends or family.

Not all lenders are going to be good

Choose your lender wisely when taking out a loan in an entity's name. Some lenders can deal with these applications without any extra hassle; others will make it very hard work, asking a lot of questions and taking a long time to muddle their way through. Some lenders won't even consider it – they'll refer you to their business banking department, which will try to charge you higher rates and fees, so run a mile.

Product options for loans in a company, trust or super fund name can vary dramatically between lenders. Some lenders will restrict features such as offset accounts (beware of this, as it's very common) and others will charge higher rates and fees. The reason for this is that historically 'mum and dad' investors typically were not that sophisticated and rarely used entities, so these loans were dealt with by business banking departments. Over time this has changed, but some banks do take a while to catch up.

> *People are living longer than ever before, a phenomenon undoubtedly made necessary by the 30-year mortgage.* —Doug Larson

* * *

You can see that there are numerous issues to consider when you borrow to invest in property that is owned by another entity, such as a trust. Hopefully, you also now understand the importance of getting robust professional advice from all of your trusted advisers, including your financial adviser, lawyers, accountants and mortgage brokers. Everyone's situation is different, and this creates different issues. As Gordon Gecko said in the 1980s movie *Wall Street*, 'The most valuable commodity in the world is information'.

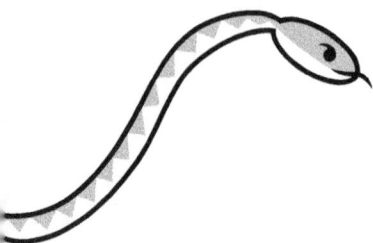

7.
TAX MATTERS

Many investors elect to invest in the residential property market for tax benefits alone: I often hear people say, 'I need to buy an investment property because I'm paying too much tax!' There are even proponents of positive cash flow and negative gearing strategies in the industry who base their methods solely on saving tax to build wealth. Chasing tax savings alone, however, will never make you independently wealthy.

Furthermore, you can't structure a transaction solely or predominantly to obtain a tax benefit, because it's against the law – the anti-avoidance provisions contained in Part IVA of the *Income Tax Assessment Act 1936*, to be precise. In this book, I discuss the consequences of certain transactions or approaches and ignore the possible purposes behind these actions, as they're likely to be different for everyone. However, before you implement any transactions, ensure that you're clear about your dominant purpose – and that it's not to obtain tax benefits. If you're concerned about whether your intensions could be misconstrued by the tax office, it's best to document your thoughts in a file note.

Having said that, it is important to maximise tax benefits (within the scope of the law), so you don't simply give away the wealth you create to the taxman. Structuring your loans and choosing the right investment strategy is important; it's also vital that you know how you'll approach the taxation side of things before you begin. After all, property investing is like building a business that can, at different times, make profits and losses. At the end of the day, your property-investment 'business' needs to generate a profit to be viable and successful.

The only difference between a tax man and a taxidermist is that the taxidermist leaves the skin.
—Mark Twain

You only get one go at it

How you elect to finance your property when you purchase it needs to be nothing less than perfect – because once you've made your choice and have set up your loans, you can never get the decision back again. If you decide you've got it all wrong, essentially, you're stuck with your mistakes (i.e. inefficient tax outcomes) as they're often too costly to fix.

So, it's important to do a lot of research and/or obtain professional advice before you jump in the deep end, to ensure you structure your investments and related loans correctly. You need to plan ahead and really think about flexibility for the future, your long-term goals and what you ultimately hope to achieve, because you only get one go at it.

A common mistake that investors make is injecting too much of their own capital into a property purchase and borrowing too little. Let's look at an example.

Example

Let's assume you buy a house for $800,000 (with a total purchase cost of $845,000 including stamp duty, and so on) and decide to contribute $200,000 in cash from a recent inheritance and borrow the rest (i.e. $645,000).

This means that the maximum tax-deductible loan you can ever claim in respect to that property is $645,000. You can't decide to increase your loan balance to, say, $750,000 down the track and start claiming a deduction on that higher balance. To put it in other words, because you contributed that lump sum of cash initially, you can't 're-gear' the property or 're-borrow' against the property and make the extra debt deductible in respect to that property – unless you change the ownership structure or use the money for other deductible purposes.

In this scenario, if you wanted to claim a higher deduction, you'd need to have borrowed $845,000 from the outset (and deposited your $200k cash in an offset – more on this later).

This simple example illustrates how important it is to know what you're doing before you start, because when you buy an investment property, you only get one chance to determine the maximum deduction you can have against it, according to how much you borrow.

If you think you only need to borrow $645,000 for that $800,000 home, but would like the option of pulling out another $50,000 down the track – perhaps to reinvest or for some other reason – there are ways and means to go about it so that you maintain some flexibility in your financial structure for the future. More on this later in the chapter.

Applicants and security don't always matter

Aside from the belief that you can 'try again' if you get your finances wrong initially, the second biggest misconception in terms of your portfolio's tax deductibility is that it doesn't really matter who applies for the loan.

If you're investing within a family unit such as you and your spouse, whether the loan is in joint names or just one spouse's name may not have any bearing on who is entitled to the tax deductions associated with that loan. From the perspective of the Australian Taxation Office (ATO), in a marital situation, the main determining factor regarding deductibility is who owns the asset in question – i.e. whose name is on the title – and who has been making the repayments.

For example, if the investment property is in the husband's name but the loan is in joint names, and repayments are being made from a bank account that is solely in the husband's name, the husband should be entitled to 100 per cent of the tax deduction (Taxation Ruling TR 93/32).

It's preferable (and cleaner) if you can arrange for the name(s) on the loan to match the name(s) on the title, as this eliminates any doubt. However, some lenders' policies or procedures might make this difficult or costly (in terms of time or legal costs). Compromising and taking out a joint loan (in the name of both spouses, for example) to acquire an investment property that's owned 100 per cent by one spouse is acceptable, as long as all loan repayments are made from an account solely in the owner's name. This account should also receive the rental income.

It's wise to document why the loan has been established in this way – that is, because the bank declined to set up the loan solely in the owner's name. To be super-careful, it may also be wise to draw up a one-page loan agreement between the two spouses, stipulating that, for example, the wife will on-lend her 50 per cent portion of the loan to her husband to use to invest in his property. (Joint applicants are assumed to own equal shares of a loan.) The wife will charge the husband the same amount of interest the bank charges her, so her tax position is unchanged – same money in as out – and the husband claims 100 per cent of the interest deduction.

I see joint loans being repaid from joint accounts but which relate to an investment in one spouse's name all the time. It's a pretty common mistake and it can end up being very costly. The ATO could argue that since both of you have been repaying the loan, the deduction should be split. However, since only one partner receives the rental income (and owns the asset), they will deny that partner a deduction for their 50 per cent of the interest cost.

It's important to note that the property used to secure a loan has no bearing on its tax treatment whatsoever. For example, you could have an investment loan secured by your home and it would still be tax-deductible. The purpose for which the funds are used, who's been making the repayments and the name on the loan will determine the tax-deductibility.

Purpose is king

Ultimately, the biggest determining factor as to whether interest is tax-deductible is the purpose for which the loan funds are used. This is what the ATO looks at in the first instance. If the item being financed is used for a purpose which has a direct relationship with earning assessable income (such as rental income and capital gains), then any interest charged in respect to the loan which finances that item should be tax-deductible. The next questions the ATO asks are who owns the investment and who's been making the repayments – the answers determine who is eligible to claim the deduction. So, if you established a loan to purchase an investment property which earns an assessable income, and one spouse owns 100 per cent of that investment property and makes the repayments, then that spouse is 100 per cent entitled to the deduction.

Sometimes people ask, 'Should I borrow against my investment property to repay my home loan?' The answer is always 'no', because it comes back to the purpose test. The purpose of the new loan would be to repay the home loan, which is a non-deductible purpose.

Don't mix loan purposes!

There are lots of reasons not to use one loan for multiple purposes – that is, to use part of the loan to invest in property and part to invest in shares. The main reason is that it makes record keeping difficult and therefore puts tax deductions at risk (because it weakens your justification for claiming a tax deduction). Another reason is that it can become a nightmare should you want to repay only part of the loan. The rule is that any repayment to a loan must be apportioned across the whole loan. Here's an example to illustrate this.

Example

Assume you have a $160,000 investment loan. Of this amount, $120,000 relates to an investment property and $40,000 was used to invest in shares. You decide to sell the shares and want to repay the loan, so you deposit $40,000 into the $160,000 loan, reducing its balance to $120,000. However, the ATO will argue that you must split the $40,000 repayment. Since 75 per cent of the loan is used for property investing, 75 per cent of the repayment ($30,000) will reduce that amount and only 25 per cent ($10,000) will reduce the share position. This can be a real pain – because you didn't want to repay the property portion. You would probably split out this loan prior to making any repayments; or alternatively, take my advice and don't mix loan purposes at all.

Redraw: be careful!

As discussed in chapter 4, redraw is the ability to withdraw any extra repayments that you make on a loan: that is, any repayment over and above the required minimum repayment. In the case of an interest-only loan, for example, the available redraw would be any principal repayment you've made during the interest-only term (as no principal repayments are required). For a principal and interest loan, the redraw amount available is any repayment made over and above the minimum principal and interest repayment.

The ATO treats any redraw as a separate loan, and once again, its tax-deductibility comes back to the purpose test. For example, say that a client has a $300,000 investment loan and receives a $20,000 bonus from work. They intend to use the bonus to take a holiday at the end of the year, and so they park the $20,000 in their investment loan in the interim to save interest. This will be considered an extra repayment. If they then redraw the $20,000 at the end of the year to fund their holiday as planned, the ATO will deem that they now have two loans – one for $280,000, which is still tax-deductible (being the balance prior to the redraw), and one for $20,000. This latter amount is no longer tax-deductible, as the loan's purpose was to finance a holiday, which has no connection with assessable income.

So essentially, when you repay a loan, you can deny yourself a future tax deduction, as you can't simply redraw the loan back up to the original amount. You need to be careful about how you use redraw facilities and what you use any redraw money for, as it can really confuse a loan balance and may end up costing you from a taxation perspective.

If, on the other hand, the client used the $20,000 to purchase another investment property, this would of course be tax-deductible. In this situation, it's important to keep adequate documentation to identify what part of that loan is attributable to what property. So, if $20,000 is used for a deposit, records need to be kept to show that the $280,000 loan is attributable to one property and the $20,000 redraw is attributable to another. However, it's best not to mix purposes in one loan.

If you really must redraw from an investment loan – to use as a deposit for an investment property, for example – make sure there's a clean audit trail, as well. That is, redraw from the loan and then transfer (ETF) the monies into the real estate agent's trust account (to pay the deposit) on the same date. Leaving redrawn money in a transaction account for weeks will weaken the audit trail and may compromise future deductions.

PLAYING TO WIN

Avoid using redraw with investment loans and be very careful repaying loans. Each redraw is treated as a separate loan by the ATO, and could affect the tax-deductibility.

Line of credit chaos

As I wrote in chapter 4, I would suggest that there are very limited situations in which a line of credit is a good product to use. One of the downsides to a line of credit, when it comes to taxation, is that it can fail to differentiate what part of the loan balance is deductible, because of the redraw situation. A line of credit is really two accounts rolled into one – a loan and transaction account. People can deposit funds into it and withdraw funds out of it with great ease.

The following example illustrates why lines of credit can become messy.

Example

Jan uses her line of credit to fund an investment property. She then has rental income paid into it, but doesn't want to use all that income to repay her loan: she pulls some out for a non-deductible purpose (to buy a car) and then decides to pay a bit more in later.

Because there are so many transactions going in and out of Jan's line of credit, the ATO must scrutinise every one of these to determine whether the total loan balance remains deductible. It can become quite confusing to work out whether monies transacting through the account are tax-deductible and whether they have an overall impact on the tax-effectiveness of the loan.

Under no circumstances should you use an investment line-of-credit account for your everyday income and expenditure. In other words, don't have your salary paid into a line of credit and pay for personal expenses from it. If you do have a line of credit, only use it for investment activities, otherwise you can get yourself into all sorts of trouble with the taxman. Parking cash in a line of credit is also not advisable because, once again, you're repaying the loan balance and then redrawing, which creates that redraw issue with the ATO.

Keep a proper paper trail

As with any business, it's vital to keep a proper paper trail when you own investment property. It's no good scrambling to get all your receipts and bits and pieces together at the end of the financial year, as the scraps of paperwork you've dug up may not adequately reveal your whole story to the taxman.

You really need to be making clear, concise notes and keeping track of all loan balances and transactions related to your investments throughout the year. If you do get audited, it's handy to be able to go back to your notes and calculations to prove and demonstrate exactly how you arrived at a particular tax deduction and/or what that amount was used for. This is particularly relevant when you're paying deposits and related expenses for properties from your loan account. What is clear to you today won't be as clear in five to ten years' time, so good record keeping will help a lot.

Let's say you have an investment account and a personal cheque account and have to pay a deposit for another property. If you transfer those deposit monies from your investment account into your personal cheque account and it's there for only one day before you write a bank or personal cheque for the deposit, that's nice and clean. The ATO can clearly see those funds going in one day and out the next – there's no confusion.

However, if you transfer that deposit amount out into your personal cheque account and the funds sit there for two or three weeks, getting mixed up among other transactions, you start to lose the audit trail. This could potentially cause you to be denied a legitimate deduction, as the ATO might question whether you funded the deposit from your own monies. Remember, the onus is on you, the taxpayer, to prove that an expense is deductible.

It's essential to keep notes at the time you make the transactions, too. It's all very well to say you'll catch up with the paperwork at tax time, but then you'll have to go back through your statements, and it can become very confusing as to which transaction was which. It's easy to put off doing your filing and making notes, but be disciplined and ensure you keep up to date, or you might forget why and how you completed a particular transaction.

If the bank makes an error with a transaction, such as withdrawing money from the wrong account or funding a loan incorrectly, you can generally 'unwind' and correct the problem from a taxation perspective. You'll need to have some sort of documentary evidence to show that they made the mistake, however – whether it's a letter from the bank or mortgage broker or a file note you make outlining who you spoke to and how they rectified the issue. There just needs to be something in your records about what happened and how it was resolved, and you should always try to resolve any such issue in a reasonably timely manner. You would probably come under fire from the ATO, for example, if your lender funded a loan for $50,000 instead of $60,000 and you only picked it up six months later, at which time they reversed it. If it's something you pick up straight away, have the lender rectify in a couple of days and keep concise file notes on the situation, the ATO will be more likely to accept your position.

Buying and borrowing costs: the good news

The good news is that pretty much all borrowing costs are tax-deductible. Any costs under $100 are deductible in the year that they're incurred and any costs over $100 are deductible equally over the term of the loan or five years, whichever is less. As almost all mortgage terms are longer than five years, borrowing costs are deductible over the first five years of the loan.

Deductible costs can include expenses at time of purchase, such as application fees, title search fees, the lender's legal fees, valuations, mortgage insurance, mortgage stamp duty, loan repayment insurance, settlement fees, security or guarantee fees. Basically, any third-party fees that are payable up-front, whether they're government or bank charges, can be deductible.

If you refinance or repay your loan earlier than the five-year period, you can claim the balance of the expense which you haven't claimed a deduction for yet. For instance, if you paid a $500 application fee and you've claimed $100 each year for three years, and you pay the loan out at the end of the third year with an outstanding cost of $200 to claim, you can claim this amount at the end of that third year.

If you establish a loan part way through the year, you'll have to apportion your claim depending on what proportion of the year you've had that loan for. So, if you take the loan out halfway through the financial year, in December, you have to initially divide the claimable expense by five to calculate your per annum entitlement, and then you halve that amount for the first year, as you'll only have had the loan for six months.

Obviously, the interest charged on an investment loan is tax-deductible – as long as it has a direct connection with the financing of that particular asset and with earning assessable income. Most lenders provide a year-end summary and statement for each loan which records and calculates the interest charges on the account.

If the loan account is used for a couple of different purposes, you'll have to apportion the interest charged on the account. For example, if you had a $300,000 loan, of which $45,000 was used to invest in shares and the rest ($255,000) was used to invest in property, 85 per cent of the interest would be claimed against the property and the rest against your share investments. However, you are reliant on your own records in this kind of situation, and it's generally better to have every loan separated by purpose and asset. This is particularly important if you have both shares and property.

If you have one loan that you withdraw multiple deposits from, however, you don't necessarily need to split that up, because with multiple properties your accounts can become too cumbersome. You should try to find a reasonable balance with some of your split accounts, though, just so you can keep track of which loan is attributable to which property or properties.

> *Next to being shot at and missed, nothing is quite as satisfying as an income tax refund.* —F.J. Raymond

Prepayment propaganda

Many lenders allow borrowers to prepay interest 12 months in advance. The benefit of prepaying the year's interest in, say, June is that you can potentially claim two years of interest costs in one tax year. That is, you claim the interest that you have paid already on a monthly basis. Then, just before the end of the financial year in June, you prepay the next 12 months of interest in advance and claim that as well, in the same year.

If you had a variable-rate loan and wanted to start prepaying interest, you would first be required to switch to a fixed-rate product that incorporated such a feature. The reason for this is that the lender has to calculate the amount of interest you need to prepay (for the next 12 months) and that can only be done if the interest rate is fixed.

Prepaying interest is normally a good strategy for people who expect to have a higher taxable income in one year compared to the following year. For example, if your usual income is $100,000, then at time of writing, your top marginal tax rate is 39 per cent (including the Medicare levy). However, if this year your income is, say, $250,000, then any amount over $180,000 will attract a tax rate of 47 per cent. So, you might decide to prepay interest to maximise your tax deduction, in order to reduce your taxable income below $180,000 (because an amount below $180,000 attracts your usual rate of 39 per cent).

However, if your income is relatively consistent year-on-year and you're not expecting any big breaks from the taxman, there's no real benefit to prepaying interest. Essentially, by doing so, you're just paying an expense to the bank earlier than is required – and in reality, most people wouldn't have such a cash surplus sitting around, because they don't receive large lump sums of rental payment or other income.

In fact, you can end up chasing your tail when you attempt to prepay interest in this manner. If you prepay one year, then you'll have to do the same thing the following year in order to get another decent deduction. The whole thing can become a vicious cycle.

Not all lenders allow interest payments to be made in advance, so if this is something you feel you can take advantage of, make sure you double-check with your mortgage provider. Many lenders who promote this option will provide a discount for paying in advance, generally of around 0.2 per cent off their published fixed rates at the time. They also often promote special rates in June each year – just before the end of the financial year.

Ultimately, whether you decide to prepay or not is entirely up to you and dependent on your financial ability to make such a large one-off payment in a particular financial year. Just be aware that you may not benefit from a taxation point of view if your income is as regular as clockwork. Do the sums and make sure the potential advantages of choosing to prepay interest will outweigh any negative repercussions in the future.

Get it right or re-gear

Another common mistake is repaying a loan only to regret it later. It's a mistake because once you've repaid your loan (i.e. reduced the balance) it changes the tax nature of the debt; and if you redraw the monies, it's treated as a new loan, as explained earlier.

So, if you've made either of these property-investment mistakes, how can you fix your mistake for the future? Unfortunately, there is no quick fix. The only way you can really undo what you've done is to change the ownership of the property and then change how you're going to pay for that asset. This is known as 're-gearing' your investment.

In the situation we considered earlier, where the husband owns 100 per cent of an asset, he could sell the property to his wife in order to get out of such a predicament. This could end up costing them dearly, however. In some states you may not have to pay stamp duty for transfers of ownership between spouses; however, you do have to pay up in others. Then there's capital gains tax (CGT). If the property was not your principal place of residence but an investment, the husband who initially owned the property will crystallise a CGT liability when he sells that asset to his wife (assuming the asset has risen in value). Capital gains tax is payable on 50 per cent of the profit at the taxpayer's marginal tax rate.

However, suppose a couple purchased a home worth, say, $500,000, spent ten years repaying their loan and then decided they wanted to upgrade to a new home and keep their existing property as an investment. Transferring the ownership and paying the stamp duty might be worthwhile in this situation, as it would allow them to rebalance their deductible and non-deductible debt. (Of course, they must get professional advice on this point.) If they don't do this, they would have to borrow the full cost of the new home purchase, which would be 100 per cent non-deductible debt (as all the money is used for non-income-producing purposes) and they wouldn't necessarily be optimising their tax position.

Remember my comments at the beginning of this chapter, though: you can't re-gear property solely to obtain a tax benefit. In my experience, a common purpose for re-gearing property is to address different investor risk profiles. For example, one spouse may prefer to sell their previous home to a third party to reduce the amount of money they need to borrow, but the other spouse may prefer to retain the previous home because they think it's a good investment. In this situation, the solution may be for the more risk-averse spouse to sell their share of the property to the other spouse. Tax benefits are incidental.

Offset debt, don't repay it!

The problem with repaying an investment loan (whether through regular or ad hoc repayments) is that you change the original tax nature of the debt. That is, as discussed earlier, if you redraw the money at a later stage, it will be treated as a new loan for tax purposes. It's important, therefore, to preserve the original tax-deductible loan balance, which also preserves your potential future tax benefits.

This is where having a linked offset account on your loan comes in. An offset gives you the best of both worlds – it allows you to park extra cash in it to offset the loan and reduce the amount of interest you pay, but also preserves the tax-deductible balance of that loan.

Let's consider again the example of the borrower who has a $300,000 interest-only loan and a $20,000 bonus. If they have an offset account linked to the loan, they can deposit the $20,000 in the offset. Because their loan is interest-only, their repayments will be calculated on the net balance of the offset and loan – so, on $280,000. (On a P&I loan, the repayments are based on the original loan amount, and remain fixed – you'd just be repaying more of the principal.)

This is one obvious bonus: the other benefit is that their loan balance never changes from the original $300,000. This means that the borrower can withdraw that $20,000 out of the offset at the end of the year to spend on his holiday without altering his ability to claim a deduction on the $300,000 loan balance. The tax-deductible loan balance is preserved.

So, an interest-only offset account (the abbreviated term for an interest-only loan with an offset) is a highly beneficial product from a tax-planning perspective, particularly if you have a lot of cash to contribute to an investment property. For instance, you might have enough cash to pay 50 per cent of the property's purchase price, but you may be better off borrowing 80 per cent (the maximum you can generally borrow without mortgage insurance) and then placing your remaining cash in a linked offset account. In this way, you still only pay interest on 50 per cent of the property's value, but you've crystallised a higher tax-deductible loan.

The bonus is that if you ever need to pull that extra cash out of the offset to use for a non-deductible purpose in the future, you can do so in a more tax-effective manner. Sure, you'll be charged interest on whatever amount you withdraw, as this amount will no longer be offsetting your loan account, but the important thing is that you preserve that lump sum tax-deductible loan amount (because you might want to utilise that sometime in the future).

By comparison, if you contributed all of the cash you had into the property initially, and then perhaps there was an emergency and you needed to access, say, $20,000, the only way to do it would be to borrow the $20,000 back – creating new, non-deductible debt.

An interest-only offset is a good place to accumulate regular cash savings. Many clients go through a few phases in their investment journey. The first phase is acquisition – acquiring their property investments. Once that's done, the next phase is consolidation, perhaps using some cash flow to reduce debt. I always tell my clients that they should never repay debt during this phase, however – they should offset it instead. This notionally reduces debt and therefore interest costs, but also builds a large holding of liquid cash, which can be very handy.

Another situation in which an interest-only offset can be of benefit is if you're purchasing a property to occupy in the short term but intend to hold it as a long-term asset. You might buy your first home, for example, live in it for a couple of years and then retain it as an investment property. In this scenario, if you have an interest-only offset and want to reduce your non-deductible debt as much as possible while you're living in the property (always a good strategy), instead of repaying the loan, all you need to do is accumulate your savings in the offset account. Again, this means you minimise the interest on your loan while preserving the original, tax-deductible balance.

Then, in two years when you decide to move out of the property and upgrade, you can take whatever cash you've accumulated in the offset account and use it towards your next home purchase, and claim a higher deduction for your existing property, which is now an investment. If you'd simply repaid your loan instead, that money would essentially be gone, and you could only claim interest in respect to the remaining balance of the loan.

Interest-only offsets are a brilliant solution for many would-be investors – something to seriously consider when setting up your finances for the future!

PLAYING TO WIN

Offset debt, don't repay it. Once a loan is repaid, it's gone forever from a tax perspective. A better approach is to accumulate cash in a linked offset to preserve the loan amount. In this way, if your home ever becomes an investment property, you'll have the flexibility to use your cash savings.

Interest on interest

The question of whether 'interest on interest' is tax-deductible has been hotly debated, and was even broached in the High Court of Australia in the early 2000s (in *Commissioner of Taxation v Hart* [2004] HCA 26).

Here's the issue. Say that you have a $300,000 investment loan at 5 per cent – an interest cost of $15,000 per annum. Instead of using your income to pay the loan interest, you decide to pay it using a line of credit (LOC). You'll then be charged interest by your LOC lender on the funds you draw from the LOC (i.e. the $15,000 you use to pay the loan interest): hence creating interest on interest.

Essentially, the High Court verdict was that if you enter into this type of arrangement solely to obtain a tax benefit with a split loan rather than two separate loans, it may not be deductible. However, interest on interest in itself was determined to be a legitimate tax deduction.

The ATO has since released Tax Determination TD 2012/1. This indicates that if you capitalise interest on your investment property loan (as described above) and divert all income (including property rental income) into your home loan for the purpose of 'owning your home sooner', this arrangement could be caught by the 'anti-avoidance' tax provisions. Essentially, the ATO would decline the deduction.

Therefore, in my view, borrowing to fund the holding costs of your investment property is probably 'aggressive' from a taxation-planning perspective and could get you into trouble.

Be prepared to pay

There are two reasons to visit your accountant. The most obvious – and something that people generally only consider once a year – is for the preparation of your tax return. Many people are prepared to pay for this service in the hope that they'll walk away with a decent return, particularly if they own an investment property and have extra income and expenses to calculate.

The other thing an accountant will do is to provide taxation advice about how you should set up and fund your property investments. This is of the utmost importance and I highly recommend you be prepared to pay for it. Don't be tempted to 'shop around' for an accountant based on fees. This is one area where you want to make sure they know their stuff – you should be comparing accountants on how knowledgeable and experienced they are in this particular field, not their hourly rate.

Make sure the advice you receive is objective, too – in other words, ask yourself whether the adviser has any vested interests. If an accountant pushes certain products under your nose before you've even got your foot in the door, alarm bells should start ringing!

In the long run, often the most expensive advice is free advice. Listening to family and friends tell you how to structure your portfolio or loans could end up costing you a lot in the long run.

There are no words that can emphasise how important it is to obtain astute, professional advice up-front and always, always avoid the armchair experts.

Of course, make sure anyone offering you tax advice (be it an accountant, financial adviser, mortgage broker or buyers' agent) is a registered tax agent. If they're not, while they might be well-meaning, they shouldn't be giving tax advice and you shouldn't be following it. You can check whether an adviser is a registered tax agent on the government Tax Practitioners Board website, www.tpb.gov.au. Of course, make sure they have lots of property-investment experience, too!

When it comes to financial and tax advice, trying to save yourself a penny or two at the start can end up costing you thousands of dollars down the track... never skimp on your future financial peace of mind!

PLAYING TO LOSE

A common mistake that borrowers make is mixing the purpose and type of debt. Always keep tax-deductible and non-deductible debt in separate accounts and, where possible, also separate loan accounts by purpose (e.g. have a separate loan account for each property).

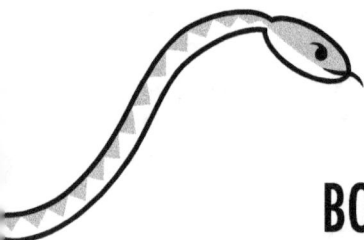

8.

BORROWING MORE THAN 80 PER CENT OF A PROPERTY'S VALUE

We looked at how much you can and should borrow in chapters 2 and 3. What percentage of an investment property's value should you borrow? With so many loan products on the market today and the option to borrow up to 95 per cent of a property's value, this is an important consideration. Remember, most borrowers will have to pay lenders mortgage insurance (LMI) if their loan-to-valuation ratio (LVR) is more than 80 per cent.

Many in the finance industry will recommend that investors and home buyers borrow a maximum of 80 per cent of a property's value in order to avoid paying mortgage insurance, as this can be costly. However, if we assume an investor's long-term goal is to build wealth, many may be better off borrowing a larger percentage of a property's value and potentially buying a better-quality property, despite the cost of LMI. So, we need to consider whether the cost of mortgage insurance is really that material in the long run.

Let's take a closer look at these issues and the pros and cons of borrowing over and above the 'magical' 80 per cent mark.

A refresher on lenders mortgage insurance

It might seem as if we're covering old ground here, but to refresh your memory, let's quickly revise and expand on the concept of mortgage insurance.

Mortgage insurance is an insurance contract (linked to a credit/ loan contract) that's arranged by the lender when an applicant borrows more than 80 per cent of a property's value. Almost all lenders use external mortgage insurance companies – and on occasion, a lender will use more than one company. There are only two mortgage insurance companies in Australia, QBE and Genworth Financial.

Mortgage insurance insures the lender's risk – not the borrower's – of a potential shortfall between the loan amount and the net proceeds from selling the property (the security). It only comes into play if the borrower defaults on their mortgage and the lender takes possession of the property and sells it. If the net proceeds from the sale are less than the outstanding loan amount, the lender may suffer a loss. The lender can then recover any shortfall from the mortgage insurer. In reality, a relatively small number of mortgage insurance contracts are acted upon.

Lenders will only insist on the client paying for mortgage insurance when they lend more than 80 per cent of a property's value, as these loans represent a greater risk – particularly where lenders extend a very high proportion of the property's value, say 90 to 95 per cent. A few lenders may lend up to 85 per cent of a property's value without mortgage insurance, but it's not common.

First-time home buyers might be able to avoid the cost of mortgage insurance, however, as I'll discuss in chapter 11.

Mortgage insurance premiums are calculated based on a percentage of the loan amount. These premiums (or percentages) increase as the loan-to-valuation ratio and the loan amount increase. Premiums can vary greatly among lenders, often fluctuating by several thousands of dollars.

The table below (which also appeared in chapter 1) sets out the typically premium ranges (excluding stamp duty) at certain loan amounts and LVRs. Of course, these rates are indicative only.

LVR	$500,000	$750,000	$1,000,000
85%	1.00–1.20%	1.15–1.40%	1.20–1.40%
90%	2.40–2.80%	2.15–2.70%	2.15–2.60%
95%	2.96–3.40%	4.00–4.70%	4.00–4.70%

To calculate how much mortgage insurance will cost, you need to multiply the loan amount by the premium percentage and then add government stamp duty, which varies from state to state but is generally around 11 per cent. (The ACT and New South Wales no longer charge stamp duty on LMI, however.) For example, assume you're borrowing $700,000 and the LVR is 90 per cent. The mortgage insurance premium would be calculated as follows, assuming the loan is arranged in Victoria and the stamp duty rate in Victoria is approximately 10 per cent:

$$\$700{,}000 \times 2.6\% \text{ (lender's premium rate)} \times 111\% = \$20{,}202$$

The mortgage insurance premium can normally be added to the loan amount – this is often referred to as 'capitalising mortgage insurance'. Some lenders will capitalise mortgage insurance over and above the maximum LVR; for instance, they may lend up to

95 per cent plus mortgage insurance up to a maximum of 97 per cent. This is normally only available to owner-occupiers, not investors.

If a loan requires mortgage insurance, the application may end up going through two approval processes, as mentioned in chapter 1. First, the lender will perform its assessment to confirm that the application conforms to its credit policies. If the lender is happy with the application, it will then refer it to the mortgage insurer for approval. Sometimes the mortgage insurer's policies can be more stringent than the lender's, particularly in terms of property location, employment stability and the types of income they'll consider. In some circumstances, applications don't always have to be approved individually by the mortgage insurer – the lender has the authority to approve them on behalf of the insurer. This is often referred to as an 'open policy'.

There are also a handful of lenders who will consider waiving mortgage insurance altogether for financially strong applicants. This is generally only an option with the larger (balance sheet) lenders and where your LVR is in the range of 80 to 85 per cent. In this instance, the lender may ask for an accelerated repayment program so that your LVR will be reduced to 80 per cent within a couple of years. This option won't be offered to you unless you ask about it – if you don't ask, you won't know!

Money is better than poverty, if only for financial reasons. —Woody Allen

How much above 80 per cent can you borrow?

Mortgage insurers will generally consider lending owner-occupiers up to 95 per cent of a property's value (plus mortgage insurance in some cases, up to a maximum of 97 per cent), with a maximum loan amount of generally $750,000. If you need to borrow more than $750,000, lenders will generally prefer an LVR of 90 per cent or less.

Investors can also borrow up to 95 per cent, but this option is typically only offered by mortgage managers and non-conforming lenders (see chapter 1 for a discussion of these lenders), not mainstream banks. Mainstream banks typically restrict investor LVRs to 90 per cent or less.

Mortgage insurers' policies are often postcode-driven. They may lend less than 95 per cent (and lower maximum loan amounts) for properties located in certain postcodes – generally where the city or town population is less than 10,000. You can check for postcode restrictions on the QBE and Genworth websites, at www.qbe.com/lmi/lenders/tools/location-wizard and www.genworth.com.au/borrower.

Prior to the global financial crisis of 2008, a handful of lenders in Australia were lending up to 100 per cent of a property's value. I doubt we'll ever see a return of that practice in Australia.

Is mortgage insurance tax-deductible?

Lenders mortgage insurance is classified as a borrowing cost, and because it will always be in excess of $100, investors are entitled to claim it as a deduction equally over five years or the term of the loan – whichever is less. For example, if you pay mortgage insurance costs of $5,000, you're entitled to claim a deduction of $1,000 per year for five years.

As always, obtain independent taxation advice to ensure that the LMI is deductible in your specific situation. Structuring your loans effectively to ensure the total LMI premiums are deductible is also important.

PLAYING TO WIN

Try to avoid lenders mortgage insurance where possible; however, never rule out borrowing extra just because it might incur mortgage insurance. Mortgage insurance can be very worthwhile in some circumstances, as it allows you to purchase more property, quicker.

So, is mortgage insurance worth it?

Although LMI can represent a considerable cost for investors, there are some situations in which it can prove beneficial. Let's look at an example.

Example

Ryan is just starting out and owns his home, which is worth $650,000, with an existing mortgage of $420,000. Ryan has two options when it comes to financing his first investment property.

Option 1: Borrow up to 80 per cent and avoid the cost of LMI

Ryan could increase the amount of lending secured by his home to 80 per cent of its current value, providing him with access to an extra $100,000. (Eighty per cent of $650k is $520k, minus the existing mortgage of $420k equals $100k.) He could use this to fund a 20 per cent deposit plus costs for a new investment property valued at $380,000, assuming that purchase costs will equate to 5.2 per cent of the property's value. In summary, Ryan will finance his investment as follows. His overall LVR will be approximately 80 per cent, so he avoids the cost of LMI.

Purchase price	$380,000
Costs (stamp duty + legal, 5.2%)	$20,000
Deposit (from loan increase)	($100,000)
Loan required	$300,000
LVR	79%

Option 2: Borrow more than 80 per cent and pay for mortgage insurance

Ryan could increase the amount of lending he used to purchase the new investment property to 90 per cent. This would allow him to purchase an investment property for up to $625,000. The figures would stack up like this:

Purchase price	$625,000
Costs (stamp duty + legal, 5.7%)	$36,000
Deposit (from loan increase)	($100,000)
Loan	$561,000
LMI	$13,000
Total loan amount	$574,000
LVR including LMI	92%

The benefit of borrowing more and paying for LMI is twofold. Firstly, it allows you to invest more money sooner, allowing you to benefit from compounding capital growth. Secondly, your higher budget will allow you to purchase a better-quality investment (e.g. located in a better area), and in the long run, this should result in a higher capital growth rate. I've compared the two options in the following table. I estimate that borrowing more and paying LMI could nearly double the dollar value of the equity you have in a property after ten years.

Scenario	Purchase price	Growth rate	Projected value in 10 years	Equity
Borrow 80%	$380,000	5.5% p.a.	$650,000	$350,000
Borrow 92%	$625,000	7% p.a.	$1,230,000	$656,000
Difference				$306,000

Mortgage insurance cost Ryan $13,000 pre-tax, but he can claim a tax deduction for this expense (over five years), so the after-tax cost is close to $8,000. And that LMI has allowed him to generate more than $300,000 of additional equity in a property. That is a good return on investment. Imagine the difference after 20 and 30 years!

Don't dismiss the idea

Many investors dismiss the idea of borrowing more and taking on mortgage insurance, considering it an avoidable expense. This may be true, but you could be limiting your investment potential by taking the option off the table.

Purchasing more property over the next five years, as opposed to waiting indefinitely, could make a huge difference to your financial position in the long term. In the example, if Ryan purchased the more expensive property, he would have accumulated over $300,000 more equity after ten years. After 20 years, the equity differential would balloon to more than $1 million. When you look at it in that light, the additional $8,000 after-tax cost doesn't seem like all that much, does it?

All I'm suggesting is that you keep an open mind. Remember your investment strategy and think long term, don't just dismiss paying for mortgage insurance as a waste of money.

A word of warning

Having said that, although the potential upsides to taking out LMI may seem tempting, bear in mind that borrowing a larger proportion of a property's value comes with increased risk. This is why your lender requires you to pay for LMI in the first place, after all! Your primary consideration should always be whether you're comfortable with the level of debt you choose to take on.

Consider the risk of rental vacancies, changes in your employment income, interest rate increases, and slower capital growth or even capital depreciation. This strategy is generally best reserved for income-rich, asset-poor investors, rather than those who may struggle to keep up with repayments should there be a slight change in circumstances.

At all times, your ability to meet repayments is an absolutely critical factor. As long as you can service the debt, borrowing a higher proportion of a property's value should pay dividends in the long term. However, if you'll struggle to make repayments and may have to sell one of the properties in the short term, you risk crystallising a loss (due to the up-front costs such as stamp duty and LMI). Do your sums and don't push yourself too far, too quickly.

Pre-approval pays

If you do decide that taking out a larger loan could be the way to go, I can't stress enough the importance of obtaining a pre-approval before purchasing a property. The need for mortgage insurance can increase the complexity and length of the loan-approval process, so the more work you can do up-front, the less stressful the purchasing process will be. A pre-approval doesn't take long to arrange, costs nothing and may save you lots of heartache.

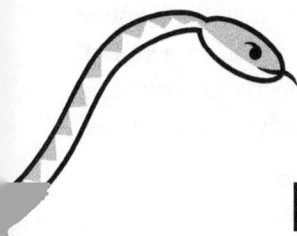

9.

BATTLING BANK VALUATIONS

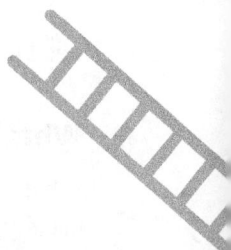

Bank valuations play a critical role in the wealth-building process, and specifically, your ability to obtain a loan for the next property you have your eye on. Consequently, they can often cause frustration, as a low valuation may delay your ability to add to your investment property portfolio. Acquiring a good understanding of the valuation process could be your best defence against this problem, as there are steps that you can take to minimise the risk of a low valuation.

As with any other financial aspect of your portfolio, remaining proactive is the best approach to this common investment issue. So, how can you take matters into your own hands and help the banks help you? Let's consider how the valuation process works and the role you can take to make the process easier and the outcome more favourable for you.

Why do banks order a valuation?

We've talked a lot throughout this book about loan-to-valuation ratios (LVRs). Banks will lend a percentage of the value of a property – and the 'value' of a property isn't necessarily what the purchaser pays for it, but what the bank values it at. So, if you're buying a property for $600,000 and apply for a loan with an LVR of 80 per cent, but the bank values the property at $580,000, you'll need to fund more than 20 per cent out of your own pocket.

A bank usually values a property at its own expense, not yours. However, as we discuss later, there may be occasions when you need to get your own valuation too.

What's a property worth and why?

What is value and how is it determined? 'Fair market value' is usually defined as a value at which a property can change hands between a willing and knowledgeable buyer and a willing and knowledgeable seller who are under no compulsion to buy or sell. This means there's no time limit on buying or selling the property. However, the definition of 'value' that banks use may differ from 'fair market value'. Some banks prefer to use a measure of value that reflects the price that would be achieved within a certain period of time – say, two months. More on this later in the chapter.

When undertaking a valuation, valuers will look for evidence to support it. That is, the valuer will complete a search (using various databases) for completed sales of comparable properties in the location surrounding the subject property. The property market can change quickly, so the comparable sales need to have been completed recently: say, within the past six months (12 months at most). Older sales may no longer provide good evidence of current value, so it really depends on what's happening in the market. Valuers are quick to adjust their opinion in a downward-moving market and slower to adjust valuations up in a rising market, as they want to ensure any recovery will be sustained before being more optimistic with their valuation estimate.

Valuers won't be influenced by properties that are 'on the market' or by 'quoted' private sales. They can only consider completed sales (i.e. unconditional sales).

When determining if a property is comparable to the subject property, the valuer will consider things like location, size of land, size and condition of property, any special features, and so forth. Two properties are rarely identical, though, so there's a fair bit of subjectivity in property valuations. In fact, valuations should more correctly be expressed as a range (for example, the value could be in the range of $750,000 to $780,000), rather than as one figure, to reflect the level of uncertainty or subjectivity that exists. However, the bank needs to work off one figure, so property valuers are in the unfortunate position of having to arrive at one figure. My guess is that that figure is likely to fall within the lower half of the valuation range – hence, many people label bank valuations as 'conservative' – which they can be.

Often, valuers work in defined geographical areas, and so they should have a good working knowledge of the local market and the real estate agents who operate in that market. A valuer will normally spend the whole day driving from property to property, taking notes and photos. They may have to complete many valuations in one day, so they don't normally spend a lot of time at each property. At the end of the day, they return to the office to complete the comparable sales research and write up reports.

Money frees you from doing things you dislike.
Since I dislike doing nearly everything, money is handy.
—Groucho Marx

Different types of valuation

There are three common types of valuation, each reflecting a differing level of research:

1. **A full valuation.** As the name suggests, a full valuation is comprehensive. The valuer undertakes a physical inspection of the property, including an internal inspection, which will also normally entail measuring the land and internal living areas and taking internal photos. Mortgage insurers generally require full valuations.

2. **A kerbside valuation.** Again, it's not hard to guess that this involves the valuer driving past the subject property, without undertaking an internal inspection.

3. **A desktop or automated valuation.** For this, the valuer collects comparable sales data based on a description of the subject property (size of land, number and size of bedrooms, etc.), without any physical inspection or sighting of the subject property. Often these types of valuations are completed using software tools.

Bank valuation policies

Valuation policies have changed quite a bit since the global financial crisis (GFC). Prior to the GFC, many lenders were trying to reduce the number of full valuations undertaken and ordering more desktop or kerbside valuations instead, to reduce costs. However, the banks' concerns about the possibility of depressed property prices (as had occurred in the UK and USA), increased their reliance on full valuations. Some lenders also started ordering valuations on all of an applicant's properties, regardless whether these properties were the subject of the loan application.

Many lenders also tightened up internal controls around the ordering of valuations. In fact, most lenders outsource the management of valuation ordering to a third party. This means that bank staff can't find out which valuation firm the bank will use in certain areas, and can't speak to the valuer before the valuation is completed (perhaps to provide sales evidence and the like). The purpose of these changes is to stop bank staff or mortgage brokers unduly 'influencing' a valuer.

The type of valuation (full, kerbside or desktop) that a bank will order depends on the loan application. If, for example, you're seeking to borrow a low proportion of the property's value and you're an existing customer of the bank, they'll probably order a kerbside or desktop valuation. If you're borrowing over 80 per cent of the property's value, however, the bank will almost always order a full valuation.

Most lenders would prefer not to revalue properties more often than once every 12 months. However, if there's a specific reason the value of a property has altered – for example, if you've completed some renovations – then most banks will be open to revaluation.

Low valuations

There are many reasons why a valuation might come in lower than you expect. For example:

- You (the owner or prospective purchaser) may have an unrealistic expectation of what the property is worth. It's common for your objectivity to be impaired in regard to a property that you have a vested (emotional) interest in.
- There may be very few sales for the valuer to rely upon to draw comparisons. In this circumstance, the valuer is likely to be even more conservative with their value estimate.
- The average time taken to sell a property could be too long. In some country areas, it can take three to six months to sell a property. A lender won't want to wait six months to sell a property, so they'll want a valuer to provide a valuation which reflects a quicker sales period.

- It may be a case of human error resulting in a poor valuation. Maybe it's been a 'rush job' or maybe the valuer is inexperienced, but poor-quality valuations do occur. Luckily, this isn't common. But, when it happens, it's very frustrating.

What can you do to maximise your valuation?

There are a few things you can do to avoid a valuation coming in below your expectations. The most important thing to do is research comparable sales yourself. Several websites, including Domain and Realestate.com.au, provide property sales data. However, a lot of this data is neither complete nor accurate, so be careful solely relying on it. You can also buy reports online from vendors such as CoreLogic (corelogic.com.au), and some banks offer property reports which you can request online. ANZ, for example, offers Property Profile Report.

Also, you can speak to a local real estate agent or the agent who manages your property (if it's an investment). They'll tell you what they think, but more importantly, many agents are happy to print off a list of comparable sales from their system, for free! You can then work your way through the list and pick those that are most relevant – that is, most similar to the property you're trying to value.

When determining if a property is comparable, you should focus first on the land size, as that's probably going to be the biggest driver of value. The next things to look at are the size of the dwelling, the number of bedrooms, the age of the dwelling, and so on. Try to remain as impartial as possible, and don't cherrypick sales results that support the maximum value. You have to give the most weight to the most comparable and most recent sales – even if the sales results don't help your cause!

Another option is to commission your own valuation. Residential valuations normally cost around $300 to $500; make sure you tell the valuer that the valuation will be used for mortgage purposes. This will give you an impartial opinion, but with more control over the process, as you'll be able to speak to the valuer yourself. However, the bank will still want to order its own valuation: it won't rely on yours.

When estimating the value of your properties on a loan-application form, you should provide a high but still reasonable estimate. You don't want to go too high, because then the valuer or lender is likely to totally ignore your estimate. However, there's no point in going too low either.

Some properties will benefit from a full valuation, particularly if they're in good condition inside or have been recently renovated. However, sometimes you'll be better off with a kerbside valuation if the property is in poor condition inside, because, obviously, the valuer won't see the inside. Sometimes, borrowers might manipulate the system to order a certain valuation. For example, if you want the lender to order a full valuation, you might apply to borrow more than 80 per cent of the property's value – remember, lenders will generally order a full valuation if the application involves mortgage insurance. Once the valuation is completed, you can adjust the loan amount down to 80 per cent. That's one way to get the valuation you want if initial requests for a full valuation are declined.

The presentation of a property can make a difference to the valuation outcome, too. So, make sure your property is well presented: lawns mowed, clean and tidy inside, uncluttered and so on. The appearance of DIY renovations can also reduce valuations.

If you consider the bank's valuation to be low, you can challenge it. To do that, you need to provide the lender (who in turn approaches the valuer) with new evidence of sales to support your estimate of value. If the difference between your estimate and the actual valuation is less than 10 per cent, though, you'll probably have very little chance of changing the valuation. If the difference is larger, you'll need two to three comparable sales which support your highest estimate to have any chance of changing the valuation. In my experience, however, it's very difficult to change a valuation, even if its inaccuracy is obvious. Often, the simplest and quickest solution is to approach a new lender, so that (hopefully) a different valuation firm is used.

PLAYING TO WIN

Research property values before lodging a loan application, and make sure you have a very good idea of what your property or properties are worth before the bank undertakes a valuation. Think about providing comparable sales data to the bank to ensure you maximise your valuations.

Be strategic with revaluations

As we discussed in chapter 5, it's important to set up your loans on a standalone basis, without cross-securitisation. The benefit of doing this is that you can revalue different properties at different times. If you notice a lot of good comparable sales occurring that support a high value, it might be a good time to revalue a property – and different locations will perform differently at different times. As such, it may not be wise to revalue all your properties all at the same time. Instead, be strategic. Revalue property when the data suggests it's a good time to do it, and increase your loan limits to an 80 per cent LVR to lock in the increased equity. This is a good thing to do, even if you don't have any immediate need for the additional borrowings.

Should you be influenced by the valuation?

If you're buying a property and your lender values it at less than what you've agreed to pay, should you withdraw from the contract or offer?

Many years ago, we were assisting a client who purchased a property off-the-plan for $2.4 million. We had the apartment valued three times, by three different valuers. One valuation came in at $1.25 million (yes, nearly half of the purchase price!), one at $2 million and one at $2.4 million. Which were wrong, and which was right? Who knows!

If I were purchasing a property and received a bank valuation for less than the purchase price, I'd investigate further, but it might not be enough in itself to cause me to withdraw from the purchase. If you purchased the property at a competitive auction, for example, then you must have been the winning bidder. By definition, there must have been a 'losing bidder' – someone prepared to pay a similar amount to you for the property. This is strong evidence of value: a property is worth whatever the market is willing to pay for it. That said, of course, in rare situations, a property auction can get out of control and egos can lead to people 'overpaying' for a property.

Bank valuations are critical

Maximising bank valuations is critical when building a property portfolio, as they can make or break your ability to purchase another investment property. Have clear and realistic expectations of your bank's valuer. Do your homework. Maintain objectivity. If you still feel that the bank's valuations are unrealistic, consider looking at other lenders. Being able to invest in an additional property could make you a lot more money than a refinance will cost you. I know that from my own experience.

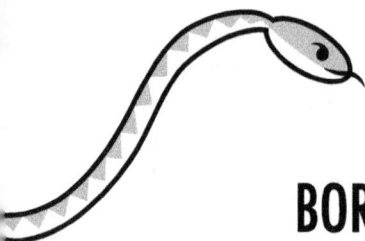

10.
BORROWING BUDDIES

Property is a hot topic at many a backyard barbecue and dinner party. Given the volatility of the stock market (there's twice as much volatility in shares compared to residential property), more and more investors are looking to property to secure their financial futures. Also, most people's superannuation is already invested in the share market, so investing in property is a way of diversifying. Property affordability continues to be cause for concern, however, and so 'partnering up' to get a slice of the action is increasing in popularity.

There are numerous reasons investors might want to consider taking on a 'borrowing buddy' to invest in real estate. Property prices in capital cities have dramatically increased over the last few decades. Finding the time to undertake adequate research to find the right investment is more and more difficult in our time-poor society. The list goes on.

Of course, this plan of attack can have as many drawbacks as potential benefits, and we all know the old warnings about mixing finances with friends and family. As an investor, you're essentially building a real estate–based business. So how does that business reconcile with a partnership structure that involves friends and/or loved ones? Is it possible to buddy up with an investment partner and still maintain a healthy relationship? If so, how do you do it?

The buddy blues

Any number of business books will tell you that partnerships are more likely to fail than succeed. While this may seem like a pessimistic viewpoint, I could not agree more, having learned the hard way from my own experiences. The good news, though, is that investing partnerships are not nearly as complex as business partnerships, and so they have a better chance of survival.

Of course, to increase your chances of success, these partnerships cannot be the result of excessive alcohol consumption with your mate on a Saturday night at the pub. They must be conceived in the cold light of day and without any rose-coloured glasses affecting your judgement. You need to approach the partnership with the premise that it's likely to fail and that you'll have to do everything possible just to make it survive. If you do this, you'll probably have a good chance of making it work. Partnerships can be very rewarding, but the majority require a lot of toil and truck-loads of patience.

One of the most successful business moguls of our time, Sir Richard Branson, always suggests a 50/50 partnership is best, because then each party has equal incentive to make it work. On the other hand, there are other businesspeople (Siimon Reynolds for one) who suggest that the contribution of each partner is very rarely equal and that's why 50/50 partnerships don't take.

Confusing as it may seem, I agree with both views, in that there is no easy way to make partnerships work. Perhaps the best thing you can do is recognise that the contribution made by each partner can never truly be equal and, in fact, this can be of benefit to both of you. For instance, a wealthy, time-poor person might be a good partner for a not-so-wealthy person with plenty of time to burn. Perhaps, at the end of the day, partnerships work better when the partners' contributions are uneven. That way, the partners need and rely on each other equally and it all works out in the wash!

Sometimes, a positive attitude is the key to success. The thought that perseverance can get you anywhere can indeed end up taking you all the way to your goal. However, I believe the reverse is true with partnerships. When conceiving the partnership, you should always play devil's advocate and think about the downside. Put written agreements in place and have a contingency plan to govern what you'll do if something goes wrong, such as communication issues arising or the partnership making a loss. This type of preparation is worth its weight in gold, as the more planning and discussion you do up-front, the fewer financially detrimental disputes you'll have down the track.

Before borrowing money from a friend, decide which you need most. —American proverb

What will the lenders think?

When two or more people apply for a loan together, for the most part, banks will assess the application as an aggregate. That is, they'll add up all the applicants' combined income, commitments, assets and liabilities and assess the application as a 'group'. If the applicants can afford the loan as a group, then that will be enough to get the application approved. Typically, a bank doesn't give a great deal of consideration to each partner's share of the debt – for instance, if there were three partners, the bank would not ensure that each partner could afford one-third of the total debt. The benefit of this is that financially stronger partners are able to support the weaker partners.

If the partners are investing through a non-trading company or trust, each partner will be required to provide personal guarantees.

Some lenders, most notably Commonwealth Bank (CBA), offer products specifically aimed at investing buddies. CBA's policy is called 'Property Share'. It allows borrowers to apply for their share of the property and each party only needs to qualify for their share. This may suit borrowers who have relatively unequal borrowing capacities: one party might be able to afford to purchase, say, 70 per cent of a property while the other party can only afford the remaining 30 per cent.

Was it as good for you as it was for me?

There are many issues to consider when financing a real estate purchase that will be owned by investment partners. Most of these should be considered up-front to avoid any messy conflicts down the line. In fact, some issues are so critical that they could prohibit the partnership from investing in any property at all.

The most significant concern is that each applicant for a loan will be jointly and severally liable for the total debt. This means that each partner will be liable for 100 per cent of the debt: their liability is not limited to just their share. This creates two significant issues:

1. If your partner(s) decide to do a runner, then you're left holding the bag. You could probably sue the person and claim ownership of 100 per cent of the property, which might seem okay. What if the property has decreased in value and there's a net loss, though?

2. Joint and several liability can destroy your future individual borrowing capacity. For example, if you apply for another loan (as an individual), the lender will assume in its application assessment that you're liable for 100 per cent of the loan repayments for the partnership's debt, because that's your

legal liability – even if, in reality, repayments might be split 50/50 between partners. However, at the same time, lenders will only take into account your share of the rental income. This could mean you have no future borrowing capacity.

Another consideration when applying for a loan jointly in a partnership arrangement is how it will be treated in the event of a fallout. Say that three partners invest together and apply for a loan together, and that one partner is significantly stronger financially than the other two parties. What happens if the stronger partner decides to withdraw from the partnership, and therefore withdraw his or her name from the loan documents?

In this case, if the two remaining parties can't afford the debt by themselves, the bank will refuse to remove the third partner from the loan, and they'll be stuck with the property (and in the partnership). The only possible solutions in this scenario are to find a replacement partner (which might be difficult, given one partner wants to leave) or sell the property. Let's face it, neither solution is optimal.

Another issue is that if the partners are not relatively equal in terms of financial strength, they could face problems sourcing finance. Lenders must make sure that every borrower has a 'financial interest' in being party to the loan.

Get your own money!

A really good solution that greatly reduces risk (and probably appeals more to equity-rich investors) is for each partner to borrow their share of the money using another asset as security. For example, I recently advised two clients who were partners (and friends) and were interested in buying a $500,000 property 50/50. I advised them to each borrow $250,000 in their own name, using their homes as security. That meant the investment property wasn't used as security at all, so there were no joint liability issues and it was all nice and clean. Of course, it's not a perfectly efficient use of equity (because there's an un-geared asset), but this probably doesn't worry people who have more equity than their borrowings need.

My advice: nothing lasts forever

In nearly two decades of advising borrowers, I've never once seen an investing partnership work as a long-term solution. My number-one piece of advice is to treat every investment partnership as a short-term solution – a stepping stone.

Normally, investors get together because they're weak on equity or income. If this is the case for you, I suggest you sit down and work out what you need to do, over what time period, to get yourself standing on your own two feet. For example, you might suggest buying a property with a partner, renovating it and holding for, say, five to seven years, and then selling. This might give each partner enough deposit funds to buy property on their own.

I think this is a far better approach, because it acknowledges the key fact that nearly all investing partnerships have an expiry date. One partner is generally left wanting out (they want to move onto the next transaction), while the other party isn't ready. They end up wasting years being polite and both getting nowhere. Look at a partnership as a short-term transaction and I reckon you have a far greater chance of success.

PLAYING TO WIN

If you're considering purchasing a property with a friend, make it a shorter-term arrangement – five to ten years maximum. Also, plan ahead and manage risks by creating documented agreements. Buying property with another partner can do serious damage to your

personal borrowing capacity and might even prevent you from purchasing further property, so tread carefully!

Changing ownership

What if, after many years, one partner wants to buy another partner's share of a property? That is, one partner wants to exit the
arrangement, but the other partner wants to retain the property.
If the property is owned personally, the title will need to change –
and that will trigger stamp duty, which could be very costly (tens
of thousands of dollars). One solution is to establish a new unit
trust and purchase the property within that trust. You can still
have a fixed entitlement, because your percentage of ownership
will be based on the number of units you hold, but you can sell
units between partners and avoid stamp duty. However, these
sales will trigger capital gains tax consequences for the seller. It's
best to speak with a proactive registered tax agent to get some
advice on this prior to purchasing the property.

Put in the work and get advice

There are many other factors to consider if you're contemplat-
ing entering into an investment partnership agreement. Apart
from the lending factors I've explored, you also need to take into
account legal and taxation issues. The bottom line is, always seek
your own independent tax and legal advice before acting upon
any suggested structures.

Some people may be concerned about the cost associated with
setting up these structures – and yes, it can be costly to establish
and maintain multiple company and trust structures. However,
consider the cost of not setting these up correctly.

Investing with partners has many pros and cons, and the finance issues can be complex, but the right structure and advice can generally resolve most things. The more work you do up-front, the more likely you'll be to succeed: better still, find a reputable and experienced accountant, financial adviser, solicitor and mortgage broker and let them do the work for you!

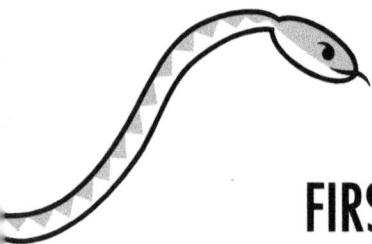

11.

FIRST-TIME PROPERTY BUYERS

Buying your first property can be both scary and exciting. It's a big decision and step in life! However, if you make a wise decision, the compounding benefits will be substantial, and the purchase will propel your financial position upward in the short, medium and long term. However, by the same token, if you make mistakes, it can be costly. The good news is that there are only a few things you must focus on, and I discuss these in this chapter.

Why this is the most important property you'll buy in your lifetime

I don't want to add to any stress or anxiety you have about buying your first property, but the fact of the matter is that this is the most important property that you'll ever buy. The reason for this is that if you buy the right property, the capital growth will help you build equity in the property, thereby strengthening your financial position. You can then use this equity towards future transactions, such as renovating, upgrading your home or investing in property or other assets.

Example

Keith and Lachlan are good mates and entered the property market at a similar time. Keith bought a new apartment close to the city in a high-rise complex for $550,000. Lachlan, on the other hand, purchased an old house approximately 15 km from the city for $545,000. They both borrowed 95 per cent of the purchase price.

Because of the seemingly endless supply of new apartments close to the city and the fact that most of the purchase price represented building value (with only a very small amount of attributable land value), Keith's property was worth $565,000 five years after he purchased it. At this point, he had $42,500 of equity in his property ($565,000 less $522,500).

Conversely, Lachlan's property benefits from its high land-value content. Also, since he purchased an older house, he was able to cosmetically improve the property, thereby adding value. Five years after he purchased it, Lachlan's property was worth $690,000, and he had $172,250 of equity ($690,000 less $517,750).

Lachlan has four times more equity in his property just because he purchased an asset with better growth prospects. He could borrow against his equity and buy a second property, or he could sell and use his substantial deposit to buy a more expensive property. He could borrow against the equity and invest the money. The point is, Lachlan has lots of options, whereas Keith has very few options because of his limited equity.

The difference between Keith and Lachlan's financial positions will become even greater as time goes on.

It's important that you educate yourself about how to identify a good (investment-grade) property from a bad one. I know this might seem like a shameless plug, but my book *Investopoly* discusses this, so if you want to learn more, I suggest you grab a copy.

Should you buy an investment or home?

Whether you should buy an investment or a home is a very common question. My answer is that it really doesn't matter, as long as you select the property using an investment lens. That is, you purchase a property with the sole (or as close to it as possible) intention of selecting a property with the highest capital growth prospects that your budget allows. Whether you then choose to occupy it mostly depends on the difference between how much rent you'll receive from the property versus how much you'd have to pay to live elsewhere. If you share a property with other people or live at home, you'll probably be better off renting out your property.

That said, it might be wise to genuinely occupy the property for a reasonable period of time in order to obtain any stamp-duty concessions on offer. These will depend on what state the property is located in: go to www.firsthome.gov.au for a link to your state's relevant page to find out more.

Trading up the property ladder

You might have a very clear picture of what your ideal property looks like – where it's located, the quality of the accommodation, and so forth. However, when you contemplate your budget, it might become clear to you that your ideal property is unaffordable.

The term 'property ladder' exists for a reason – because the easiest way to achieve your ideal property is to climb the ladder. Most people's first property is not their dream property. If your budget is limited, you might have to buy, improve and sell a couple of properties over the next decade before you'll be in a position to afford your dream home.

When are you ready to get into the market?

Two factors determine whether you're ready and able to buy your first property: cash flow and your deposit amount.

Cash flow

Do you have a stable and reliable surplus cash flow that you can contribute towards repaying a loan? There are usually two main considerations here. First, how stable and consistent your income is expected to be in the short to medium term – normally, you'll need permanent full-time employment or an established self-employed business. Second, do you have good cash-flow management and consistently spend less than you earn? In other words, are you a good saver?

Don't think that you can tighten up your cash-flow management after you've purchased a property. Firstly, as discussed in chapter 3, lenders will review your expenditure levels when assessing your loan application. If you're spending all your income, they won't approve a loan. Secondly, you need to prove to yourself that you're ready and willing to maintain (or reduce) your expenditure so that you can afford to make loan repayments.

Deposit

Do you have enough deposit to contribute towards the purchase? As discussed in chapter 8, most banks will lend up to 95 per cent of a property's value. Therefore, you need to be able to pay:

- a 5 per cent deposit
- the mortgage insurance premium (see the table in chapter 8), and
- any acquisition costs, which could include stamp duty, buyers' agent fees (if you choose to use such an agent) and legal fees.

Typically, this means that first-time buyers need to accumulate a sizeable deposit, and this can, unfortunately, take many years to save – over which time property prices will probably continue to climb. In my experience, having enough deposit is often the primary hurdle for first-time property buyers to overcome. There are two possible solutions to this:

1. Check whether you qualify for the First Home Loan Deposit Scheme (FHLD scheme).
2. Speak to your parents or other family members to see whether they'd be willing to provide a family guarantee.

The First Home Loan Deposit Scheme

The First Home Loan Deposit Scheme is a scheme introduced by the Commonwealth Government on 1 January 2020. It helps eligible borrowers who have at least a 5 per cent deposit by providing them with a guarantee for the remaining 15 per cent. This reduces the LVR to 80 per cent – allowing you to avoid lenders mortgage insurance. Your loan amount is still up to 95 per cent, but your LVR is reduced to 80 per cent because the lender holds two securities in respect to your loan: 1) your property, and 2) a guarantee from the government.

You apply to participate in the FHLD scheme via an approved lender. The scheme is only available to people who earn less than $125,000 per year, or $200,000 per year for couples. There are also property purchase-price limits, depending on the state and location of the property. Find out more by visiting the website: www.nhfic.gov.au/what-we-do/fhlds. The government will provide guarantees under the scheme for up to 10,000 Australians per year.

Family guarantees

A family guarantee is similar to the FHLD scheme, but the guarantee is provided by a family member (usually parents), not the government.

Family guarantees provide two benefits. Firstly, there's no minimum deposit required. This means that once you have a satisfactory cash flow position and can afford a loan, you can get into the property market without further delay. Secondly, it reduces your LVR to below 80 per cent, which means you avoid mortgage insurance.

A family guarantee is provided by using equity in your family's property (either in their home or investment), and it's usually limited to a dollar value. For example, let's say you want to buy a property for $600,000, but you only have $10,000 in savings. For the sake of this example, we'll ignore any costs (legal fees, stamp duty, etc.). A family guarantee loan could be structured as follows:

- You apply for a loan for $590,000 – or probably for $600,000, so you can retain your savings as a buffer.
- This loan is secured by the new property ($600,000) and a limited guarantee of, say, $150,000 provided by your family member.
- Therefore, the bank holds security worth $750,000 in total for a loan of $600,000, which is a loan-to-valuation ratio of 80 per cent.

Then, in time, when your property increases in value and is worth more than $750,000, you simply approach the bank and request that they release the family guarantee. (If they decline this request, you could simply refinance to a new lender.) Once this is done, your loan is solely secured by your property and your family is no longer on the hook.

Family guarantees have a number of pros and cons. Here are some of the pros:

- It doesn't cost your family anything except for some legal fees (the bank will want guarantors to obtain independent legal advice).

- It still puts the onus of responsibility on you to qualify for the loan using your income only.

- The property will be in your name only, avoiding any need to change the ownership in the future.

- These arrangements are typically short term. In my 18 years of experience, no family guarantee arrangement has remained in place for longer than five years. However, there are no guarantees (excuse the pun!). If the property's value remains stagnant and the loan balance doesn't reduce, the arrangement could remain in place for the whole term of the loan.

- It shouldn't impact on your parent(s) ability to downsize or upsize their home. (Please obtain personalised advice to confirm this is correct for your situation, of course.)

A few of the cons are as follows:

- If your family's property already secures an existing mortgage, you'll need to use the same lender. This means that either your family needs to refinance or you need to use their lender.

- Providing a guarantee will eat into your family's equity. They will need to take this into account if they have plans to increase their borrowings in the future.

- A family guarantee is limited in dollar terms, but practically speaking, a lender can't sell just a portion of your family's property. So, if you default on your loan and the bank sells your property for less than what you owe them, the bank will want your family to pay the shortfall. If they can't do so from their own funds, the bank will sell their property. While the guarantee amount is limited and they will keep the remaining sale funds, it doesn't change the fact that the property will be sold, and this could have consequences such as capital gains tax.

To get a clear picture of all the pros and cons that will apply in your specific situation, you must obtain independent financial, credit and legal advice before pursuing this option. For further information, you can also speak to a professional mortgage broker or lender that offers this option.

Should you use the First Home Super Saver scheme?

The First Home Super Saver scheme (FHSS) allows you to use your superannuation fund to save your deposit for your first home. You make additional super contributions (via salary sacrifice) into your super fund – these contributions are taxed at 15 per cent, as opposed to your marginal tax rate, so it will delay paying some tax. Then, once you have enough of a deposit, you can withdraw the extra contributions you've made, plus an additional amount to account for investment earnings less tax.

For more information about the FHSS, go to the ATO's website (www.ato.gov.au) and enter 'First Home Super Saver Scheme' into the search box.

The scheme is complex, and I really don't think it provides much of a benefit. It seems most Australians agree with me, because very few people have used it. I think first-time borrowers are better off pursuing either the FHLD scheme or family-guarantee options.

Understand that it's unlikely to be your 'forever' home

It's unlikely that you'll occupy the first property you buy for the rest of your life – more likely, it will be a stepping stone to your next property. There are two things you can do to accommodate this likelihood:

1. **Treat it as an investment decision rather than a lifestyle one.** That is, select the property purely for investment purposes and put your lifestyle considerations aside. That way, when it comes time to move on and upgrade, you can consider retaining your first property as an investment. Often, people do this but fail to realise that a nice home does not always make a good investment – in fact, it rarely does. Most people convince themselves that their previous home will make a good investment because they're emotionally attached to it. Emotions often cloud our judgement.

2. **Buy a property that has scope for cosmetic improvements that will add value.** This will increase the likelihood you'll enjoy some capital growth, even if you only own the property for a few years. Of course, you could benefit from general market price increases. However, if you also improve the property's value, then you're not solely reliant upon the market to lift prices.

In closing

The best time to buy your first property is as soon as your cash flow permits. If you have enough cash flow to service a loan, then you should investigate all the options discussed above and buy your first property as soon as possible. Focus on buying the best-quality property that your budget will allow and look for cost-effective ways to improve or enhance its value. Do that, and you won't regret it in the long run.

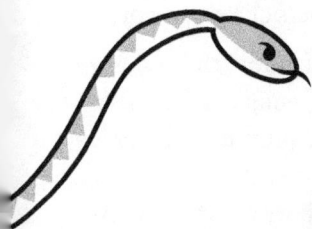

12.
DEVELOPING A FINANCING STRATEGY

Many people are at a loss when it comes to financing a property that, on paper, is negatively geared. They're uncertain how they'll make up the cash-flow shortfall that often comes with well-located, high-capital-growth property, as opposed to a high-yielding, 'pays for itself' rental investment.

On the other hand, some people never even consider starting a property investment career because they believe they simply can't afford it. They think, 'How can I possibly pay off my own home while I'm saving a deposit for another one?'

The reality is that you can have your cake and eat it too. In this chapter, I show you a winning investment strategy, based on smart borrowing! But first, I need to talk a little about equity, as this plays a vital part in building wealth through property investing.

Equity equals opportunity

Many people overlook equity when it comes to property finance. 'Equity' is the net realisable value of a property – how much cash you'd walk away with after you deduct sale costs, outstanding debt and capital gains tax from what the investment is currently worth.

However, there's another definition of equity that's very relevant when you start talking about using equity as financial leverage – 'borrowable equity'. Borrowable equity is essentially the property's value multiplied by 80 per cent (with 80 per cent representing the amount you can generally borrow without the need for mortgage insurance), minus whatever you owe against the property. For instance, if a property is worth, say, $500,000, you can theoretically borrow $400,000, but if you already owe $300,000 against the property, your borrowable equity will be only $100,000 – the extra amount you can borrow using the property as security.

The true beauty of equity is that it increases over time, isn't taxed like your hard-earned savings are, and can be used to help you climb the property ladder much faster than you can if you save cash to use for deposits on further investment purchases.

So, let's have a look at how equity can work to increase your borrowing capacity, build your portfolio and keep your cash flow on track.

Deposit power

Many people who consider getting into property investment feel that before they can make a move, they have to work their behind off to repay their home loan and become debt-free. This would be a dream come true for most of us, but the reality is, it can take a very long time to do it and, in the meantime, you could be missing out on potentially lucrative investment opportunities.

Most home owners are sitting on a goldmine, with substantial equity in their property, and they don't even know it. Equity is like the goose that lays the golden egg, in the sense that it can build on itself in a variety of ways and continue to grow and work for you.

One way that equity can increase your potential to make even more equity is by using some of the capital you have in your own home as a deposit for investment purposes. It's much easier to rely on the escalating capital in your home, rather than trying to save a deposit from scratch, for two reasons. Firstly, equity is not taxed like income (not until you sell it, anyway) and secondly, the natural growth in value of a well-placed property will far outweigh any interest you could earn via a savings account.

In other words, if you're keen to build an investment portfolio in property, you're far better off adjusting your mindset to the idea of borrowing more, rather than scrambling to pay off your home.

The key is to buy a good quality asset, then let capital growth work its magic over many years and decades, while you refinance to release borrowable equity that you can use as a deposit. There you have it – a simple way to step up the property ladder.

Anyone who lives within their means suffers from a lack of imagination. —Oscar Wilde

Loving the leverage

When it comes to equity, the more you have, the more agreeable you'll find lenders will be when it comes to handing over extra borrowings. This is because equity in a property provides them with greater loan security. Using equity in this way is known as 'leverage' and it's an excellent way to gain progress in your property-investment endeavours.

Example

Let's say that a would-be investor, William, has a home currently valued at $600,000, with a $300,000 loan – therefore, $180,000 in borrowable equity. William wants to buy an investment property for $700,000, but doesn't have a cash deposit because he's been concentrating on repaying his home loan.

In this instance, the bank will add the total loan amount that William requires and compare it to the total security he'll have. So, William's total loan will be his $300,000 existing mortgage, plus $740,000 for the purchase of the investment property ($700,000 plus $40,000 for costs). Of course, we would split these loans out to avoid cross-securitisation, but for the sake of simplicity, let's ignore this for a moment. William's borrowing more than the total cost of his new investment property and increasing his overall borrowing to $1,040,000.

At the same time, the total value of the property the bank will be holding as security is $1,300,000 (William's home, worth $600,000, and the investment property, worth $700,000). The LVR is calculated by dividing $1,040,000 (total borrowings) by $1,300,000 (total security): William's total LVR is 80 per cent.

So, although William has borrowed nearly 106 per cent of the new investment property's value (being the price plus costs), the equity in his existing home reduces his overall LVR and provides the bank with ample security.

Buying property that pays

This might all sound very promising, but there are several factors that can bring the equity equation unstuck for investors. The most crucial element to being able to access and use equity in property is the actual building of enough capital to generate adequate amounts of the stuff in the first place.

From this perspective, I can't stress enough how important asset selection is. You need to be investing in the highest quality assets, so that you maximise your chances of enjoying strong capital growth. I discuss this in detail in my book *Investopoly*. Even more importantly, you need to regularly review the performance of the properties you own. You should never settle for second-best, and so you should dispose of any underperforming properties as soon as possible. This is something the vast majority of investors don't do for many reasons: I suspect the primary motive is that they don't want to admit they picked the wrong property!

You should be looking for an average capital growth rate of 4 to 5 per cent above inflation, at the very least. Even a 1 per cent differential in capital growth will result in almost $500,000 difference in equity after 20 years (on a $750,000 property)!

That's why I believe that before you buy an investment property, you really should seek professional advice (or at least a second opinion) from a qualified, independent investment-property adviser. With so much potential wealth on the line, you'd be silly not to! Purchasing the wrong asset can be very costly in terms of stamp duty, subsequent selling costs and more importantly, lost capital growth.

From a credit perspective, lenders often consider the location of a property. If people are buying high-capital-growth properties, demand will outstrip supply and that makes lenders feel confident that they can realise that asset in a timely manner if required. In other words, if the wheels fall off and you can't make the repayments, the lender knows that they'll probably be able to sell the asset quickly and for a reasonable price.

Whoever said money can't buy happiness simply didn't know where to go shopping. —Bo Derek

Capital growth will help fund retirement

The following graph charts the value of a $750,000 investment property over 30 years, assuming it grows in value at an average rate of 7.5 per cent (which is the median house growth rate since 1980). In 30 years, the property will be worth over $6.5 million. That might be hard to fathom, but two-bedroom houses in inner-city suburbs of Melbourne were selling for $130,000 approximately 30 years ago. Today, they cost north of $1.3 million – ten times that price.

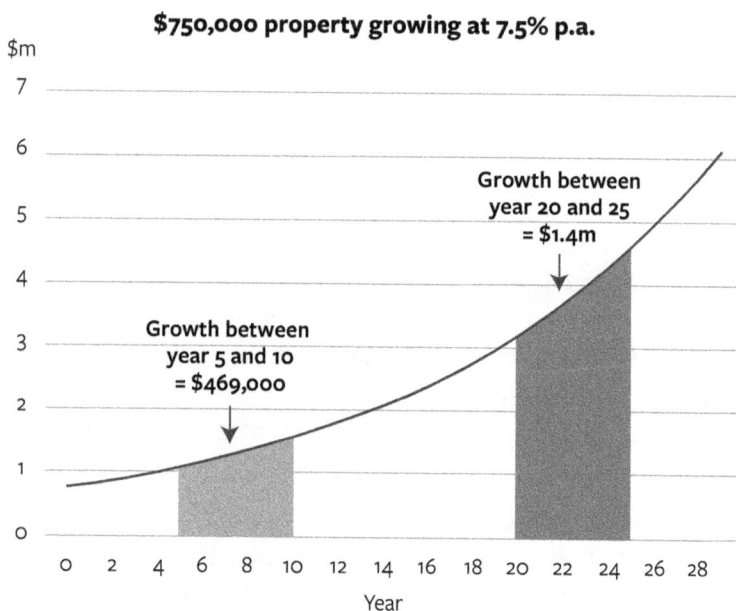

$750,000 property growing at 7.5% p.a.

Growth between year 20 and 25 = $1.4m

Growth between year 5 and 10 = $469,000

Anyway, what's interesting to note is the change in value and the power of compounding capital growth. In years 5 to 10, the property increases in value by $496,000. That sounds healthy, right? Well, look what happens between years 20 and 25 – another 5-year period. The property increases in value by $1.4 million – an average of $280,000 per year! This is the power of compounding capital growth.

Think about it this way: in 30 years' time, the investor who holds this property might still have a loan for say $800,000 (being the purchase price plus costs). However, if the property is worth over

$6.5 million, the investor has over $5.7 million in equity and an LVR of only 12 per cent! In this case, the property will be more than paying for itself – that is, its rental income will be more than all of its expenses, including interest.

Most people will have some superannuation to draw from by the time they reach age 60, but it may not be enough to last the rest of their life. So, look at it like this. Your superannuation can fund the first phase of your retirement – be it 10, 15 or more years. Then, once your super balance is nearly depleted, you can sell your investment property(s) and end up with a bunch of cash in the bank.

This is why having a financing strategy is so important. Bestselling author Michael Yardney has always said 'real estate investing is a game of finance with some houses thrown in the middle' (see 'Property investment for beginners – 10 common mistakes' at Propertyupdate.com.au). You need to have access to money such that you can safely purchase one to three high-quality properties and hold them for the long run. The main thing that's in short supply is access to money (i.e. borrowings). If you can master that, you can master property investing.

PLAYING TO WIN

Don't get spooked – they're only numbers. Some people are overly worried about taking on additional borrowings. Of course, you have to be absolutely comfortable that you can afford to take on additional debt, but don't get emotional about investing. The numbers don't lie. If your budget suggests you can afford more borrowings and you have the necessary risks managed (e.g. income-protection insurances and buffers), then go for it. Property has always seemed expensive. Thirty years ago, a $130,000 property was expensive. Don't be scared. Fortune favours the brave!

Of course, *never* borrow more than you can afford

Again, to be absolutely crystal clear, I'd never suggest to anyone that they borrow more than they can afford to repay. Doing so is foolish and invites financial hardship.

Borrowing to invest in property, like any other investment approach, is not without risks. The three main risks are interest-rate increases, a depressed rental market (no rental growth) and low capital growth.

The interest-rate risk can be addressed by fixing the interest rate on most of the debt. Selecting a top-quality property and engaging a professional property manager will minimise your vacancy and income capital-growth risks. However, the only way to account for potential risks, particularly for an absence of rental income, is to build a buffer into the loan, thereby allowing for a temporary cash-flow deficit.

How do I release my equity?

Okay, so once you've come to terms with the idea of using your equity to either start out in property investment or add to an existing portfolio, how do you actually get hold of your equity? What practical methods of 'refinancing' or 'restructuring' are the safest, and what are the pros and cons of using various loan structures to release your equity so it can work for you? We've already looked at loan structures in general, but it's a good idea to revisit them with specific regard to releasing and using equity, so you know exactly how they apply in this scenario.

Lines of credit

There's no denying that a line of credit can be a handy way to access equity, and is often recommended to investors as the easiest option. Many lenders and mortgage brokers suggest that lines of credit are beneficial because they provide borrowers with flexibility in terms of availability of funds, transaction capability and loan repayments, all at home loan rates.

It's true that a line of credit allows investors to withdraw the funds they need (up to the agreed limit) for a number of purposes – such as to put down a deposit or purchase an investment property. However, in my experience, less than 5 per cent of the clients I deal with would benefit from using a line of credit to access their equity. Generally speaking, a line of credit is more expensive than other loans, because most lenders charge a higher interest rate for them. There are many other loan products that allow you to access equity without having to pay any interest at all, until you use the money. This is of great benefit if you intend to use your equity for a deposit on an investment property, as you'll need to set up the loan facility before you make the purchase.

For this reason, I'd suggest that as an alternative to a line of credit, investors should consider a loan with redraw or an interest-only loan with an offset attached. Although a line of credit can be a good option, there are often lower cost products that allow easy access to borrowable equity.

Second mortgages or refinancing

A second mortgage is taken when an investor approaches another lender, with whom they don't have their initial mortgage, to take out a loan against their home or another property they own. For instance, if you were to decide you want to access your equity to put a deposit on another property, you might approach the Commonwealth Bank, when your initial home loan is with Westpac. You'd end up with two separate mortgages from two separate lenders against the one property: Westpac holds the first mortgage, and Commonwealth Bank has to register a second mortgage.

This isn't really a popular option these days, and most lenders avoid second mortgages wherever possible. The secondary bank is uncomfortable with such a set-up, because it knows that the initial mortgagee will be paid out first should anything go wrong – as a result, it will often lend a much lower LVR to obtain a higher security buffer. Therefore, it's not an efficient use of equity.

Generally, these days you'd refinance with the lender who already holds the mortgage on your home and establish a second account with them – this is often called an 'internal refinance' or 'restructure'. Alternatively, you'd refinance everything to a new lender and establish two new accounts – often called an 'external refinance'.

An 'internal refinance' has some distinct advantages. Your existing lender can establish a second loan account just by setting up a new loan agreement. This means they simply rewrite the existing mortgage contract, or create a totally separate mortgage contract, but generally don't need to change the registered mortgage itself, as they already have a charge over that property. They're really just using the equity in it. They would revalue the property, do the sums to work out how much borrowable equity can be released, then give you access to those funds by establishing a new account (assuming you can afford to borrow the money, of course).

When you establish a second account in this manner, you can opt for either an interest-only basic variable loan or an interest-only package-type loan with an offset facility. The basic variable loan would be fully drawn on the day it's established, and you would then take the money and repay it back into the loan, leaving a small portion outstanding (say, $100), and redraw this money as required for your deposit. With an interest-only package-type loan, you'd deposit the loan funds you can access (let's say, $100,000) into the offset account. Because the loan is offset by the $100,000 cash, no interest is payable until you withdraw the money from the offset to use as a deposit for your next investment.

An 'external refinance' can be advantageous in three common situations:

1. if your existing lender refuses to match the interest-rate discounts that other lenders are offering and therefore becomes too expensive

2. if your existing lender values your property at less than what you think it is worth (and what another lender will value it at), or

3. if your existing lender has a lower borrowing capacity and therefore is unwilling to approve more lending.

In both cases, these accounts need to be established prior to making an investment-property purchase, so that you can access the necessary deposit from your equity. It's likely that both these options will turn out to be cheaper than a line of credit.

Refinancing rules

Any secondary accounts you establish are the direct result of refinancing your existing mortgage. As we said earlier, you have two options when you refinance to gain borrowable equity: either an internal refinance from your own lender or an external refinance from another lender.

An internal refinance simply involves approaching your existing lender and restructuring your loan(s), by varying your existing loan contract. The bank will conduct a valuation on your property and tell you how much you're able to access, then establish a second account. The beauty of establishing a second account, as opposed to increasing the size of your existing loan, is that you can maintain some distinction between the purpose of the debts, which is very important. Remember, you don't want to get your non-deductible debt mixed up with your tax-deductible debt – the paperwork nightmare this creates is horrifying!

When you engage a new lender to do an external refinance, they have to do a valuation on your existing property, then contact the incumbent lender, arrange to pay them out and take over the existing mortgage, as well as establish a new account for your borrowable equity.

There's a negative and positive aspect to taking the approach of starting over with a new lender. On the downside, it can take longer than an internal refinance and could be more costly (i.e. there could be discharge fees from your existing lender) – although lenders usually offer incentives to refinance which more than offset the cost. However, if you want to access your equity to make further investments, the bank's valuation becomes critical, so using an external refinance can provide a clean slate and potentially a more favourable outcome with the valuation process.

For instance, if valuation issues arise with your existing bank – let's say because they use a very conservative valuer in your area – it can pay (literally) to approach a completely different lender who uses a different valuer. Also, you might be restricted by your current lender's valuation policy, in that some lenders will only conduct revaluations every 12 months: external refinancing is a way to get around that.

Developing a plan

As with almost everything, investing some time into developing a financing plan can be very worthwhile. Most people can't invest without finance, so it's a pretty important thing to get right, and planning can maximise your chances of success. Everyone's plan will be different, depending on their financial situation and goals, but remember, the best time to borrow is when you don't need it, so preparing loan arrangements for your next move is an advantage.

Some of the things to consider when developing your plan include:

- establishing loan arrangements prior to starting a family (as you may reduce to one income for a period of time)
- understanding what stage the property market is at and whether revaluing properties now makes sense (e.g. if the property market is very strong, it may be a good time to revalue)
- considering the type of property you're investing in and your investment strategy (for example, if you have limited equity, then it may be better for you to invest in property that will deliver some immediate equity, or equity in a short period of time – allowing you to leapfrog into another investment property)
- considering the timing of an owner-occupier purchase and its impact on potential future property investments
- making sure your loan arrangements are flexible enough to accommodate any expected changes in your personal circumstances, and the cash-flow consequences of these – both positive and negative
- being careful about repaying any loans – often, as I've mentioned before, it's better to accumulate cash in an offset to reduce or eliminate interest rather than repaying the principal.

The considerations can be endless. The best advice I can give you is to get some good professional advice and try to plan ahead as much as possible.

Creating a strategy to pay down debt for retirement

One other thing you should consider when planning is your interest-rate sensitivity in retirement. If, for example, you have $2 million of borrowings, an interest-rate increase of 1 per cent will cost you an extra $20,000 per year. Once you're retired and your only sources of income are investments and super, that extra interest could have a big impact on your cash flow and standard of living.

Generally, therefore, you want to aim for a debt level that is far less sensitive to changes in interest rates. Worrying about rates is the last thing you want to be doing in retirement!

Here are five strategies you could use to reduce your debt exposure in retirement:

1. **Buy an asset specifically to sell.** Selling assets to repay debt solves one problem (i.e. it reduces your debt), but it can create another – it may mean you have insufficient remaining investments to fund your retirement. However, if you decide from the beginning that you're going to sell an asset to reduce debt, you can proactively plan around this. Firstly, it would be wise to focus on ways to reduce your capital gains tax (CGT) liability, such as by owning the asset in a family trust, as tenants-in-common or in your super fund. Secondly, you can select the asset and location that best suits this strategy.

2. **Use surplus cash flow.** You could spend less and direct some or all of your surplus cash flow into offset accounts to notionally reduce your debt. This does two things. First, it reduces your net debt exposure and cash-flow sensitivity to changes in interest rates, and second, it improves your investment portfolio's liquidity, because you have immediate access to cash if you need it.

3. **Reduce debt so your investment properties are cash-flow neutral.** It can take decades to generate good returns from investing in property, because it generally takes at least 10 to 15 years for compounding capital growth to produce significant equity gains. So, taking the principle of strategy 2 a little further, you could deposit enough surplus cash flow into offset accounts to reduce your net debt to a level where the

rental income will pay for the property's expenses and loan interest – in other words, so the property will break even and doesn't 'cost you' anything. You could even deposit enough cash to generate a positive cash flow.

4. **Withdraw monies from super.** After age 60, you can withdraw your super tax-free. Depending on your super balance, debt exposure and other investments, it may be appropriate to withdraw funds from your super to repay debt.

5. **Downsize your home.** I'm very cautious about strategies that rely upon crystallising equity by downsizing the family home, as people might like to downsize in terms of accommodation size, but this doesn't necessarily translate to a downsize in terms of value. However, it is an option to consider.

Using a mortgage broker

Mortgage brokers often deal with 30 or more lenders, which is useful when developing a financing strategy. Brokers can work out which lenders you could use first in order to safely maximise your borrowing capacity. They can also help you ascertain what's doable borrowing-wise, and they can help you maximise your borrowable equity, since they can order up-front valuations with lenders before they even lodge an application form. Many mortgage brokers are property investors themselves, so they'll be on the same page as you and will understand what you want to achieve.

Of course, there are some great people working for the banks – very professional and knowledgeable. However, the fact of the matter is that bank staff only have access to one lender's policies, parameters and valuation panel. Virtually all investors will need to use different lenders at different stages of their investment journey, and mortgage brokers are well placed to help with that.

Just as in any industry, there are good and bad mortgage brokers. The best way to find a good broker is simply word of mouth – speak with other successful property investors and find out who they use.

Equity: your biggest asset

Obviously, as I mentioned earlier, to initiate the types of strategies I've discussed in this chapter, you must have enough equity in your existing property, and also serviceability (discussed in chapter 3). Equity is a tremendous asset, giving you the opportunity to invest without having to contribute any cash.

Some of you could be sitting on a mountain of equity and not even know it, essentially wasting a great prospect to create tremendous wealth... just because you don't know how or because you have a fear of 'spending more to make more'. My advice would be to never discount any possibilities when it comes to wealth creation via property investment. If you're really concerned, talk to an independent expert to get their take on your situation and whether you're ready to take the plunge. After all, you have nothing to lose, but potentially a whole lot of money to gain!

> *When I was young, I used to think that money was the most important thing in life. Now that I am old, I know it is.* —Oscar Wilde

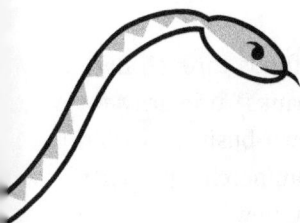

13.

CONSIDERING COMMERCIAL FINANCE

Commercial property generally has higher rental yields, so it's increasingly advertised and recommended to investors as a practical direct-investment alternative to residential property. It's true that commercial property has some excellent advantages over residential property. However, investors should be aware that the commercial-property lending market is very different to the residential lending market.

The limitations, costs and availability of commercial finance may significantly affect an investor's opportunities and the returns on their commercial investment. This is not an area for the faint-hearted to dabble in! You need a sound understanding of the financial nuts and bolts involved, as if you get the lending set-up wrong, you can end up with chronic flaws in your commercial investment portfolio.

One dollar for eternal happiness? I'd be happier with the dollar. —Monty Burns (*The Simpsons*)

Behind the eight ball

Although the commercial lending market has welcomed many new players over the past few years, it still lags somewhat behind residential finance in the diversity of products it offers and the lending policies it practises.

Historically, commercial borrowers sourced funds through first-tier lenders (such as one of the Big Four banks) primarily for owner-occupy purposes – to operate their own business within the commercial premises. However, as commercial property investment has become more popular, many new lenders have entered the arena, creating increased competition and forcing a reduction in commercial lending rates.

Generally, commercial lenders can be segregated into three categories:

1. the Big Four banks (NAB, Westpac, CBA and ANZ)
2. second-tier banks (e.g. Suncorp, St. George, Bankwest, AMP)
3. mortgage managers and specialist lenders (e.g. Judo Bank, La Trobe Financial, emoney).

As in the residential loan market, the deregulation of the banking industry had a large hand in attracting these new entrants into the commercial lending arena to generate a better range of options for consumers who can enjoy the fruits of a much more competitive playing field. New, smaller, specialist lenders are shaking up the market and delivering much-needed competition and innovation.

Residential vs commercial loans

Life would be much easier for residential investors who decide to dabble in commercial property if finance options for the two asset classes were remotely comparable – unfortunately, this is not the case. The commercial lending market differs significantly from the residential lending market, particularly in terms of credit policies and product features. Let's look at the main differences.

Lower LVR

The maximum loan-to-valuation ratio (LVR) for a commercial property is generally 70 per cent, as opposed to the residential market, where you may be able to borrow up to 95 per cent of a property's value. Having said that, a small number of commercial lenders may lend 75 per cent or even 80 per cent in some cases.

The LVR can also affect the interest rate – in other words, the higher the LVR (normally over 60 to 70 per cent), the higher the interest rate on the loan. Investors can, of course, contribute more equity in order to minimise the interest rate (by borrowing less than 60 to 70 per cent), but this is likely to reduce their returns on equity compared to what may be achievable with residential property.

The primary reason a higher LVR is such an issue is that often the success of a commercial portfolio is based not only on capital gains, but rental yields. So, if a lender provides too much capital at the outset, the investor's loan repayments are at risk of substantially exceeding any decent rent returns, rendering the investment a failure.

Furthermore, most lenders will reduce the LVR even further if the commercial property is classed as 'specialised'. 'Specialised' property – a restaurant or pub, for example – has been constructed for a specific purpose and cannot be used for any other function without modification. The pool of potential purchasers for specialised properties is substantially smaller than the pool of buyers for non-specialised properties, which means that specialised properties are more difficult to sell. Therefore, all things being equal, investors' returns on equity for specialised properties may be less than non-specialised properties due to the additional equity funds required.

Fewer loan products

Essentially, commercial lenders offer two product types:

1. basic term loans (fixed or variable)
2. lines of credit.

A basic term loan is set over a fixed term during which the borrower repays either principal and interest or interest-only. These loans have few features to speak of, and so are typically referred to as 'set and forget' arrangements. Even though more options are being introduced in this area due to increasing competition, commercial lenders generally don't offer features such as offsets, which are more commonplace in the residential lending market. Lines of credit from commercial lenders (which can be quite expensive) are very similar to the residential products, which I discussed in chapter 4.

The more you borrow, the more purchasing power you have

This is true for most things in life, but it's even more relevant in the world of commercial finance: the more you borrow, the more interest-rate-negotiation power you have. For example, some lenders offer more competitive interest rates to clients who borrow in excess of $1 million – for obvious reasons.

Shorter loan terms

Maximum loan terms for commercial loans range from 15 to 20 years (or 5 years for interest-only loans). This increases the minimum principal and interest repayments compared to residential mortgages, which generally allow for maximum terms of up to 30 years. Commercial properties are therefore more likely to be cash-flow negative on a principal and interest basis, negating that all-important rental yield.

Counting the cost

Probably the most notable distinction between residential and commercial finance is the interest rates. Commercial variable interest rates are typically 1 per cent or more higher than residential interest rates. However, sometimes commercial fixed rates can be quite attractive and similar to residential interest rates.

Many large banks' loans are priced on a case-by-case basis, depending on the individual strengths and weaknesses of the application, although some lenders do have standard 'off-the-shelf' pricing like residential lenders. The interest rate charged will be directly impacted by the lender's credit assessment. The factors taken into account when they assess the risk of a commercial loan include:

- **the property itself** – its condition, location, type, versatility, and so on
- **the strength of the tenancy** – the existing lease terms, the quality of the tenants, the history, lease options and so on
- **the interest coverage** – that is, whether the rental income covers the interest bill adequately; normally, lenders look for 1.5 times interest-only coverage
- **loan-to-valuation ratio** – as discussed earlier in the chapter
- **the financial strength of the borrower** – asset position, income capacity and creditworthiness.

In residential loan applications, approval hinges more on the strength of the borrower, but commercial lenders normally focus attention on the strengths and weaknesses of the property (the security) and the tenants.

If you owe the bank $100, that's your problem. If you owe the bank $100 million, that's the bank's problem.
—J.P. Getty

Risky business

In some cases, lenders may consider commercial loans to be higher risk prospects than residential loans. There may be a couple of reasons for this.

Firstly, the pool of potential purchasers for commercial properties is substantially smaller than for residential properties, which affects the lender's ability to sell the property in a timely way if necessary (i.e. it affects the asset's liquidity). However, perhaps this risk should be reflected in the type of valuation ordered (e.g. the lenders could seek more of a 'fire sale' valuation) or in the LVR approved rather than in the interest rate charged. Admittedly, some lenders do this, but not all.

Secondly, the risk associated with rental income can be higher than residential. Vacancy periods are often a lot longer, and often commercial properties are leased by businesses, whereas residential properties are generally occupied by PAYG employees. Therefore, the risk of a commercial tenant defaulting on rent payments may be greater, as the commercial tenant is reliant on the business operating effectively to meet their obligations. This risk obviously depends largely on the strength of the tenant – a government department or large corporate tenant, for instance, might be considered less of a risk.

Fees, fees, fees

As with most finance products, you'll typically be required to pay up-front and ongoing fees for a commercial property loan. Application or establishment fees can range from 0.25 to 1 per cent or more of the loan amount, which can be quite substantial in dollar terms. The average is approximately 0.5 per cent.

In addition, borrowers are normally required to pay the valuation and legal fees. These fees generally range from $1,500 to $3,000, depending on the value of the property and complexity of the transaction. Valuation fees can vary depending on the property type and location: for instance, specialised properties are more costly to value.

Such up-front costs can affect the financial viability of holding commercial properties on a short-term basis – a strategy commonly referred to as 'flipping' properties. Commercial lending thus better suits 'buy and hold' investment strategies.

Other fees may include:

- annual review fees
- ongoing service or line fees
- early repayment fees (i.e. break fees).

There's no standard or average cost for these fees.

So, as you can see, it's crucial to find out and consider all the extra charges you could be up for when you're calculating the overall cost of borrowing for a commercial investment.

Back to the future

So, what does the future hold for the commercial lending market? Only two decades ago, consumers had very few alternatives when it came to home loans, which were very basic products. Options such as offsets, redraw and unlimited extra repayments were unheard of, and certainly not marketed aggressively as they are nowadays. How times have changed! Today it's something of a challenge trying to keep up with the glut of new products and features that flood the residential market continuously.

The good news is, we're starting to see some progress within the commercial finance arena that indicates this market is heading in a similar direction. As a more diverse set of borrowers enter the commercial property market – 'mum and dad' investors, professional investors, owner-occupiers and so forth – and as competition and demand increase, so too will product innovation (hopefully!). It won't be long until similar products are offered for commercial property as those currently available to residential borrowers.

Commercial finance brokers

There are many commercial lenders in Australia, and many are not well-known brands. Each lender has a particular credit appetite and specialisation, and this can change regularly. Therefore, I always recommend that borrowers seek advice from a specialist commercial broker. In fact, I have some commercial loans and I use a commercial broker. It's a specialist area and, as with many things, you need to be working in it every day to be proficient.

Best of both worlds?

As I touched on at the beginning of this chapter, I think there are some great advantages to investing in commercial property. In fact, it's something we advise our financial planning clients to do once they've accumulated a strong asset base in residential property. Investing in residential property initially allows you to primarily enjoy strong capital growth rather than income (which is what you need while you're working) and allows you to leverage a smaller asset base. Once this capital growth increases your net asset base, you may be able to transition safely into the commercial market. The added benefit is the stronger income returns, which is what most people prefer (and need) as they move closer to retirement.

If you choose this approach, you may be able to enjoy the best of both worlds. That is, you can use a residential mortgage to access the equity in your residential portfolio, and use that money to invest in commercial property. Essentially, you'll be borrowing at residential interest rates to access commercial returns.

You may not have enough equity in your residential property to buy a commercial property outright, but the more residential finance you raise, the less commercial finance you need – thereby reducing the overall cost of finance. Not all lenders will be happy to give you a residential mortgage if they know you're going to use the money for commercial investment, but there are a few that are comfortable approving what lenders call 'cash out'.

For now...

Unfortunately, the reality is that commercial mortgage lending hasn't yet quite caught up with residential finance when it comes to options and the level of competition. However, commercial property is continuing to gain popularity among investors, and it's important that prospective punters understand the limitations and opportunities associated with it from a lending viewpoint. My clients are often surprised and disappointed at the differences between commercial and residential property lending. The solution: ensure you know exactly what you can (and can't) finance before you decide to go down the commercial property investment road.

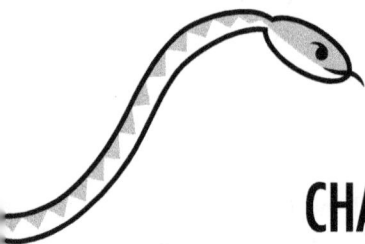

14.
CHAPTER TAKEAWAYS

Over the next few pages, I've provided summaries of the key takeaways from each chapter as a quick, easy reference for when you're arranging or rearranging your loans. They're the ultimate Rules of the Lending Game!

Why you need this book

- Lending has changed dramatically over the past few years, and you now need to start planning at least six months in advance of applying for a loan. It's important that you're well informed so you can navigate the potential challenges.

- Setting up mortgages is deceptively easy. That is, it's easy to make a costly mistake, but not realise this until several years later. A little bit of knowledge will help you avoid the common errors.

- You must understand that a mortgage is an asset; used wisely, it will help you achieve your lifestyle and financial goals. Maximising your borrowing capacity safely is key to this.

- Building wealth is a game of finance – using other people's money to help you build your own wealth. This book shows you how to win the game!

Chapter 1: The players

- The mortgage industry has evolved over many years, but the Big Four still dominate the market. There are many smaller alternatives, but be aware of their pros and cons.

- The tightening of credit practices throughout 2017 and 2018 was the most significant change since the introduction of Aussie John in the early 1990s. Understanding the current landscape will put the mortgage application and management process in perspective.

- You must understand how a lender funds its mortgages, as this will determine how flexible they'll be – and whether their flexibility is important in your situation. Matching the right lender with your application is key to success; don't try to put a square peg in a round hole.

- Mortgage insurers have a great deal of influence on loan applications where you're seeking to borrow more than around 80 per cent of a property's value. Make sure you understand and plan around lenders mortgage insurance.

- Establishing a relationship with a trusted mortgage broker can save a lot of money, time and hassle, and they'll focus on helping you achieve your lifestyle and finance goals.

Chapter 2: How much should you borrow?

- Be cautious with your borrowing plans. Wealth-building isn't a race, and it's important to borrow safely.

- It's critical that you know how much your living expenses are. Astute cash-flow management is imperative for successful wealth accumulation.

- To get a detailed understanding of your cash flow, download the past three months of your transactions and allocate them into seven categories. Analyse your spending in these categories and look for savings.

- I recommend you set up two bank accounts. One you use to receive all your income and to pay all your financial commitments. The other you use to pay living expenses from. Allocate a set amount into this second account each fortnight – and once it's gone, it's gone!

- Good cash-flow management doesn't take a lot of time and isn't a painful experience. The key aim is to reduce any unconscious spending that doesn't have a meaningful impact on your standard of living.

- Once you know how much surplus cash flow you can save, you can work out how much you should borrow.

- See page 32 for a list of steps that you should take, approximately six months out from lodging a mortgage application, to ensure that you're 'borrower-ready'.

Chapter 3: How much can you borrow?

- Three things will determine your borrowing capacity:
  1. Serviceability – which involves an assessment of your current cash flow to ascertain whether you can afford to repay the loan.
  2. Security – which relates to how much cash (skin in the game) you'll contribute towards purchasing a property and/or how much equity you have in other property. A lender must ensure you have enough assets (security) that it will at least get its money back if you stop making repayments on your loan.
  3. Creditworthiness – do you have an unblemished record of making repayments on time, not overborrowing and generally conducting yourself well?

- Different lenders may assess your borrowing capacity very differently, so it might be important for you to consider and compare a large number of lenders, either yourself or via a mortgage broker.

- For your first property purchase, if you want to borrow more than 90 per cent of a property's value, you need to have at least 5 per cent of that value in genuine savings.

- On page 44, I list 13 things you can do to maximise your borrowing capacity – including minimising credit card limits, submitting a PAYG tax variation and minimising other financial commitments.

- If you find you're struggling to make your loan repayments at any stage, take decisive action as soon as possible. This might involve making temporary changes or contacting your lender.

Chapter 4: Perusing the products

- Determine which product and structure you need first, then consider which lender provides the best solution – don't choose the lender and try to make their products work.

- It seems like there are millions of different loan options but, in reality, most borrowers only need to choose between three products: a basic variable loan, a discounted standard variable rate loan within a package or a fixed-rate product.

- Package products allow borrowers to establish multiple loan accounts and offer an interest-rate discount based on total borrowings. Packages are typically the most cost-effective products for investors.

- Data shows that fixed-rate borrowers have been financially worse off 69 per cent of the time since the year 2000. The odds are stacked against you, although that's not necessarily a reason to avoid fixed rates. However, I caution anyone about assuming they'll be better off (i.e. will pay less interest) if they choose a fixed-rate product.

- Offset accounts are valuable for borrowers who have a home loan, as it allows them to reduce the amount of (non-tax-deductible) interest they pay.

- Data published by the Reserve Bank of Australia demonstrates that banks offer new borrowers lower interest rates than existing customers. Therefore, it's important that you (or your mortgage broker) review your interest rates regularly – at least annually.

- Setting up your investment loan with interest-only repayments gives you the most flexibility. It sets the minimum repayment amount at the lowest level, thereby giving you discretion over what you do with your cash flow. If you also have an offset account against the loan, you can park cash in this, saving yourself interest.

- Loans to construct a dwelling or dwellings are more complex and are set up differently.

Chapter 5: Structuring your loan portfolio

- How you structure your loans can impact your tax deductions, your ability to make additional investments, your risk and your cash flow. So, it's important to get it right.

- The example featuring Karen and Richard, beginning on page 81, shows how to correctly structure your loans.

- You should review your loan-to-valuation ratio periodically and maintain it at as close to 80 per cent as possible to avoid giving your lender excessive security.

- Spreading your lending across multiple lenders allows you to establish a credit history with each of them, and this will likely serve you well in tighter credit markets.

- Avoiding cross-securitisation (i.e. where a loan is secured by two or more properties) provides many benefits. It can decrease property revaluation costs and increase flexibility, it allows you to maximise your borrowing capacity, puts you in a better negotiating position with lenders, means that you can enter into fixed-rate products safely, allows you to control sale funds when you sell a property, and much more.

- Fixing a broken loan structure entails splitting out loans and ensuring they stand alone. There's an example of how to do this on page 85.

- Structuring loans effectively may allow you to minimise the cost of lenders mortgage insurance.

- Getting your loans and structure pre-approved by a lender could save a lot of time and heartaches after you purchase a property.

Chapter 6: Structuring your loans in a company or family trust

- It's important to get holistic and independent advice before you decide to set up a company or trust to own your property investments, as there are many implications to consider in areas like financial planning, legalities, tax and borrowing.

- When it comes to loans in a company or trust name, lenders will typically fall into three categories: 1) they will not allow such loans; 2) they allow the loans but charge higher rates or fees and/or they're not experienced with these sorts of loans, which causes errors, frustrations and delays; or 3) they're experienced with such loans and charge standard rates and fees. Of course, it's important to select a lender from the third category.

- To access a deposit, it's important that the deposit loan is in the trust's name. You can provide a guarantee so that the lender can secure the loan using the equity in your home (or another property).

- On page 108, I shared a step-by-step example of how to structure a loan in a trust's name.

- I recommend that investors avoid using hybrid trusts for a number of reasons, including the fact that few lenders will lend to them.

- If you're considering investing in property via a super fund (an SMSF), make sure you investigate all the pros and cons carefully, as compliance obligations have tightened dramatically and only a handful of lenders offer these loans.

- Do not agree to giving a lender a registered mortgage debenture over your company or trust.

- It's very likely that the directors of a company (including a trustee company) and/or individual trustees will need to provide personal guarantees for a loan to the company or trust.

Chapter 7: Tax matters

- You only get one opportunity to establish the maximum tax-deductible loan, and that's when you first purchase a property. So, think very carefully before you contribute cash towards a purchase. If possible, borrow 100 per cent and deposit your cash in a linked offset instead.

- The property's ownership determines who gets the tax deductions; the names on the loan matter less. It's important to ensure that the loan repayments are made from an account in the owner(s) name.

- The loan purpose will determine whether it's tax-deductible or not. If the loan funds were used to buy an asset that will produce assessable income, it's likely the interest will be tax-deductible.

- Avoid using redraw facilities with investment loans, as any redraws are treated as new, separate loans for tax purposes.

- Lines of credit are very messy for tax purposes, so my general recommendation is to avoid them.

- Keep good records of when your loans were established, when the balances were changed, how loans were refinanced and so forth. These records will come in handy in years to come as your memory inevitably fades.

- Borrowing costs (bank fees) for up to $100 are deductible in the year they are incurred. Fees greater than $100 must be written off over five years.

- Prepaying interest is worthwhile if you expect your taxable income this financial year to be unusually high.

- An interest-only offset is a powerful product that allows you to reduce your interest costs without compromising future tax (interest) deductions. All investors need to be aware of this.

- Make sure you have a smart, proactive accountant who's experienced in property investing. It's good to complete last year's tax returns, but my advice is to spend the same amount of time discussing this year's tax-planning strategies.

Chapter 8: Borrowing more than 80 per cent of a property's value

- If you borrow more than 80 per cent of a property's value, you'll have to pay lenders mortgage insurance (LMI). LMI is a one-off fee payable when your loan is established.

- LMI protects the lender from suffering a loss, not the borrower.

- LMI is charged as a percentage of the loan amount. The percentage charged depends on the loan size and LVR, but ranges from 1 to 5 per cent (see the table on page 136). Most states (except NSW and the ACT) charge stamp duty of around 11 per cent on the premium amount.

- LMI is tax-deductible – claim it over five years.

- Most lenders will lend up to 95 per cent of a property's value. For investors, mainstream lenders limit the maximum LVR to 90 per cent, but there are mortgage managers and non-conforming lenders that will lend 95 per cent.

- Lenders will allow borrowers to add the LMI premium onto the loan as long as the total loan amount does not exceed a 97 per cent LVR.

- Mortgage insurers may reduce their maximum LVR depending on the property's location and type (rural towns, high-rise apartments, etc).

- Mortgage insurance can be worth paying for, because it magnifies your equity and allows you to invest more, sooner. This might help you purchase a better-quality investment property and therefore generate better investment returns in the long run. There's an example on page 140 to demonstrate this.

- If you're borrowing more than 80 per cent, your application may need to be approved by the lender and the mortgage insurer separately. Mortgage insurers can have tighter credit policies than lenders and this can add time to the loan-approval process – so it's wise to arrange a pre-approval before you purchase.

Chapter 9: Battling bank valuations

- Banks will independently value your properties when you purchase them and when you refinance or make changes to your loan.

- The difference between a good and bad valuation could make or break your investment plans: a bad valuation will retard your ability to implement your investment strategy.

- To determine a value, valuers will search for sales of properties that are comparable to yours. The sales must have occurred recently – in the last 6 months, or 12 months at most.
- There are three types of valuations: full, kerbside and desktop valuations. Depending on the state of your dwelling (i.e. how it presents), one type might be more favourable than the others.
- Low valuations can occur in four situations:
  1. You have an unrealistic impression of your property's value.
  2. There might not be enough comparable sales (as in 2018 and 2019, when sales volumes were at all-time lows).
  3. Properties in some locations take a lot longer to sell, so the bank will determine a value that will achieve a quick sale (this isn't very common).
  4. The valuation was of poor quality.
- While it is possible to challenge a bank valuation, it's rarely successful. So, if you get a low valuation, often the most expedient thing to do is switch to a different lender.
- You can do two things to maximise value:
  1. Keep on top of past sales data to ensure you have a realistic idea of what your property is worth. There are a number of online tools you can use (see the chapter for details) and your property manager should be able to help, too.
  2. Be strategic when you request a revaluation. Don't necessarily wait until you need to borrow more money – revalue property when there are plenty of helpful comparable sales.
- Maximising valuations is an important step in building a property portfolio. Be prepared to switch to a different lender if they give you a higher valuation. Most mortgage brokers are able to order free valuations with multiple lenders.

Chapter 10: Borrowing buddies

- Investing in property with a family member or friend will help you pool your borrowing capacity, but it's not without risk. Documenting such arrangements will help you navigate the inevitable changes in circumstances and markets.

- Typically, when two or more people apply for a loan together, lenders will aggregate their income and expenses in order to determine their overall borrowing capacity. However, some lenders' policies and products allow each partner to apply for their share of the loan separately.

- The most notable risk with a partnership is that each borrower is jointly and severally liable for the total debt. This means that if one partner stops making repayments, the remaining partner(s) are legally responsible for making all repayments.

- Buying property with a partner will have a negative impact on your personal borrowing capacity, as lenders will normally account for 100 per cent of the debt but only your share of the income from a partially owned asset. This can materially decrease your standalone borrowing capacity.

- One solution for avoiding the joint and several liability issues is to raise your own funds separately; for example, you might borrow against an existing asset to fund your share of the acquisition.

- The best way to approach joint borrowing is to understand that it's a shorter-term arrangement – lasting, say, 5 to 10 years – and planning accordingly.

- Owning the property in a unit trust may perhaps assist partners to change ownership percentages in the future without incurring stamp duty. You must obtain professional taxation advice in this regard, however.

Chapter 11: First-time property buyers

- The first property that you buy is arguably the most important, because if you select it well and it increases in value, it'll create more opportunities for you to build wealth sooner – and the compounding benefits of this can be enormous.

- It's not important whether your first property is a home or investment. Selecting it as if it *were* an investment (i.e. making sure it has the strongest investment attributes) is the key thing.

- Understand that, depending on your current financial strength, you may have to trade your way up the property ladder to your dream home – that is, you may need to buy, improve and sell a few times.

- Two things determine whether you're ready to buy your first property: firstly, you need to have a stable and reliable surplus cash flow to make loan repayments with, and secondly, you need to have a sufficient deposit.

- You may be able to use either a family guarantee or the First Home Loan Deposit Scheme to assist you if you're income-rich but deposit-poor.

- Understand that your first property is unlikely to be your 'forever' home, and therefore, employing an investment approach (and ignoring lifestyle considerations as much as possible) will serve you well.

- Getting into the property market as soon as it's safe and prudent to do so is typically a good financial decision, particularly if you plan to purchase an investment-grade asset.

Chapter 12: Developing a financing strategy

- A well-known Australian property adviser says that property investment is a game of finance rather than real estate.

The reason for that is that borrowing capacity is a scarce resource, and if you can maximise it, you can afford to safely invest in more property and therefore build more wealth.

- It's far more efficient to build your property portfolio by funding your property deposits from equity than by saving after-tax dollars. You must proactively maximise borrowable equity in order to achieve this.

- Compounding capital growth will do all the heavy lifting in the long run – that's why it's absolutely critical to select the best investment-grade property you can afford. Get advice in respect to this.

- Debt is a wonderful servant but a terrible master, so always borrow within safe limits. Building wealth is a marathon, not a sprint!

- The best product to use to access equity is a variable loan in a package with interest-only repayments and an offset account.

- There are two types of refinance: internal (with the same bank) and external (with a different bank). The most important factor will likely be the valuation – go with the lender that gives you the highest valuation.

- You should develop a financing plan that sets out how you can maximise your borrowing capacity and successfully implement your property investment strategy.

- You must consider how you will repay debt or at least reduce it to a manageable level after you retire. I shared five strategies for doing this on page 182.

- An experienced, professional and ethical mortgage broker can help you safely maximise your borrowing capacity and your borrowable equity, by comparing valuations from multiple lenders, if necessary.

Chapter 13: Considering commercial finance

- Commercial mortgage products are very different to residential mortgages. They typically have less features.

- Commercial LVRs are lower than residential LVRs: normally, the maximum LVR is 70 per cent.

- Commercial loan terms are shorter, too – the maximum is typically 15 years.

- Commercial loan applications are assessed primarily on the strength of the commercial asset, with less emphasis on the borrower. Considerations include the type of property, the LVR and the strength of the tenant and lease.

- Commercial property fees can be a lot higher, with application fees ranging from 0.25 to 1 per cent. Borrowers must pay for valuations.

- If you want to purchase a commercial property and you have a lot of equity in your residential properties, sometimes it's best to use a residential loan to raise borrowings to fund a commercial acquisition. However, this depends greatly on your circumstances.

- Given that the commercial lending market includes many fringe lenders that have niche specialisations, it's best to engage the services of a commercial broker, as they'll likely save you a lot of time, hassle and money.

APPENDIX:
CREDIT POLICIES

Smart borrowers understand that education and research give them an edge. This appendix sets out the security most lenders will require and the income they'll look for from a borrower to qualify for a loan, at time of writing. Of course, each lender has its own credit policies, dictating how a loan application is assessed and what is and isn't considered suitable security and income to service a loan. It's impossible to document every lender's policies, so I've endeavoured to set out the 'average' policies.

This information is not exhaustive and lending policies change regularly, so it's extremely important to check with individual lenders.

Acceptable security

The following table sets out the average acceptable security for various types of property.

Security/property type	Maximum LVR without LMI	Maximum LVR with LMI
Residential dwellings – house detached, semidetached, terrace, duplex townhouse, villa, strata title holiday home zoned residential	80%	95% + LMI up to 97% (max. loan is $1.15 m)
Vacant land	80%	95%
Community title	80%	90% – 95%
Company title	80%	95% in a capital city
Moiety title	70%	Not generally acceptable
Display homes	80% (most lenders)	Up to 95%
Stratum title	80% (most lenders)	Not generally acceptable
Converted commercial	60% – 80% (not all lenders)	Case by case
Converted industrial	60% – 80% (not all lenders)	Generally, not acceptable
Serviced apartment, holiday apartment or resort apartment	60% – 80% (very few lenders)	Generally, not acceptable
National Rental Affordability Scheme (NRAS) properties	80%	90%
Living area less than 50 m² (exc. balcony and car park)	60% – 80% (very few lenders)	Up to 90% if more than 40 m²
Transportable homes (once utilities are connected)	70% – 80%	95% (some lenders)

Security/property type	Maximum LVR without LMI	Maximum LVR with LMI
Licensed builder – fixed-price contract	80%	95% + LMI up to 97% (max. loan is $1.15 m)
Owner-builder	60% – 80% (very few lenders)	Not acceptable
Non-resident applicants	70% – 80%	Not acceptable
Properties worth more than $3 m	Some lenders will reduce LVR to 70% – 75%	Max. loan for LMI is typically $2 m
Mining towns (certain postcodes)	70% – 80%	Generally, not acceptable
Vacant land zoned rural	Generally, up to 70%	Not acceptable
Rural residential or residential greater than 50 hectares	Not generally acceptable	Not acceptable
Retirement village accommodation	Not acceptable	Not acceptable
Timeshare property	Not acceptable	Not acceptable
Property located in inner city (high density)	80%	80%
Property located in town with population of less than 10,000	80%	Case by case
Crown leasehold property (remaining lease term is greater than loan term)	60% – 80%	95%
Up to 3 dwellings on one title	80%	Case by case

Security/property type	Maximum LVR without LMI	Maximum LVR with LMI
Up to 4 dwellings on one title	70%	Not acceptable
5 or more dwellings on one title	Not generally acceptable (need commercial loan)	Not acceptable

Acceptable income

This next table provides guidelines on what income is regarded as acceptable and gives lenders confidence that the loan will be repaid.

Income	Policy
Salary and wage (permanent part-time and full-time)	100% of income
If it's a new employer and your probationary period has not been completed	If you are in a similar role and in the same occupational role, most lenders will consider including 100% of your income. Otherwise, you must complete the probationary period.
Bonuses	80% as long as there are 2 years of history
Overtime	80% (3 to 6 months of history is required)
Commission	80% (3 to 6 months of history is required)
Second job	Generally, 100% if ongoing

Income	Policy
Self-employed income	100% (a least 1 full year's trading results reflected in tax return, with most lenders requiring 2 years of history)
Family Tax Benefit	100%
Super pension (industry fund/ SMSF pension or indexed pension)	80% – 100%
Casual job	100% if you have 6 months of consistent history
Rental income	70% – 80% of gross amount
Interest and dividend	Up to 80% if supported by tax returns (normally 2 years of history)
Centrelink payments	Only considered if it's supplementary income
Child maintenance/support	80% – 100% with 6 months of history

If there is anyone to whom I owe money, I'm prepared to forget it if they are. —Errol Flynn

GLOSSARY

Borrowable equity. Borrowable equity is essentially the property's value multiplied by the percentage amount that a lender is comfortable to lend (typically 80 per cent, as this is the amount you can generally borrow without the need for mortgage insurance), minus whatever you owe against the property.

Borrowing capacity. Your borrowing capacity is the amount a lender will lend you. If you already have short-term loans, credit-card debt or other property loans, your borrowing capacity will be reduced.

Break costs. Also called 'exit fees'. These are the costs a lender will charge if you pay out your loan early, perhaps to take out a loan with a more competitive lender. The government legislated in 2011 to reduce the levels of break fees. It is now only legal to charge break fees that are a reasonable reflection of the lender's costs. So fees still do exist, mainly for basic products and fixed-rate mortgages.

Building societies. Similar to banks, building societies are cooperative organisations that accept deposits of money from savers and use them to make loans, secured by mortgages, to property buyers. They generally offer all the services of a regular bank, but during the GFC they did not offer the government-backed security.

Capital adequacy. This is the amount of capital (equity) the bank has compared to its risk weighted assets (assets being cash, mortgages, other loans, etc.). Capital adequacy is used to measure a bank's ability to meet its liabilities and other risks. Australia has very strict rules around capital adequacy to ensure its banks remain robust.

Capital gains tax (CGT). Tax payable on the profits from the sale of investments.

Credit unions. See also *building societies*. Credit unions are cooperative financial institutions that are owned and controlled by their members and operated for the purpose of promoting savings, providing credit at competitive rates, and providing other financial services to their members.

Creditworthiness. This is a creditor's measure of an individual's or company's ability to meet debt obligations (i.e. repay a loan).

Cross-securitisation. Where a loan is reliant upon more than one property as *security*.

Discretionary trusts. Also known as *family trusts*. Discretionary trusts are structures that are formed to operate a business or to be used as an investment vehicle. The trustees of a family trust operate the trust according to its rules (contained in the *trust deed*) and act in the interest of all beneficiaries, determining how the capital and income from the trust will be distributed.

Dividend. A dividend is an income distribution made by a company to its shareholders. Dividends are usually expressed as a number of cents per share. Many companies listed on the stock exchange pay dividends twice each year, usually a smaller 'interim' dividend and a larger 'final' dividend.

Encumbrance. An encumbrance, as it pertains to real estate, means anything that burdens title to the property, such as a mortgage (loan), an easement or a restriction that limits the title (caveat).

Equity. Equity is the net realisable value of a property – how much cash you walk away with when you deduct sale costs, outstanding debt and capital gains tax from what the investment is currently worth.

Family trusts. See also *discretionary trusts*. A family trust is a discretionary trust set up to manage investments and/or a company and distribute profits to family members.

Gearing. Also see *leverage*. The extent to which an investor or business is using borrowed money. For example, if an investor's portfolio is 'highly geared', he or she will have taken out loan(s) to fund a high proportion of the assets.

Global financial crisis (GFC). This is the label that has been given to the period between 2008 and 2009 which saw the collapse of large financial institutions in the US and parts of Europe, resulting in bailouts by national governments, and downturns in stock markets around the world. Also referred to as the 'credit crunch', it was a difficult time to borrow money.

Guarantee. This is the agreement a guarantor gives to a lending institution, which includes the obligation to fulfil the terms of the loan contract (i.e. make repayments) in the event that the borrower(s) default.

Guarantor. A person or company acting as a third party that endorses an agreement to guarantee that a loan will be repaid. Under such an agreement, the guarantor is liable for the loan should the principal party to the loan (the borrower) default. If a trust or SMSF borrows funds, an individual or company will usually be required to be a guarantor to secure these borrowings.

Hybrid discretionary trust. This is a trust structure which combines the features of two different kinds of trusts: a discretionary (family) trust and a unit trust.

Interest-only loan. With an interest-only loan, the borrower is only obliged to pay the interest on the loan each month (without repaying any of the principal). Interest-only loans can free up cash flow for an investor who is confident that the property's capital growth will ensure that the principal is easily repaid when the property is sold, providing additional profit as well.

Lenders mortgage insurance (LMI). Borrowers who borrow more than 80 per cent of the value of an asset will usually have to pay lenders mortgage insurance. This additional cost can amount to thousands of dollars. In some cases, smart structuring of loans can minimise or avoid this cost.

Leverage. See *gearing*. The extent to which an investor or business is using borrowed money.

Loan-to-valuation ratio (LVR). This is a ratio which measures the loan amount as a percentage of the property's value. For example, if the LVR on an investment property is 80 per cent and the property is valued at $400,000, the lender will advance $320,000 and the borrower must fund $80,000 of the investment.

Margin (e.g. interest-rate margin). The difference between cost and income. For example, banks make their margin by paying a lower interest for funds on deposit than they charge on the funds they lend to borrowers.

Margin lending. Lending funds to individuals to enable them to borrow money to invest in listed shares or managed funds. The amount of funds loaned is based upon the amount of assets held by the borrower, which are pledged as collateral on the loan.

Mature. To end or complete. When a loan term ends or a fixed-interest period finishes, they are said to have matured.

Moeity title. A title to property where the owner owns a share of the total land on the title and leases a certain portion of the land back for themselves from the other owner(s). Typically applies to maisonettes or attached cottages.

Mortgage. A registered charge over property given by the owner (borrower/mortgagor) to a lender (mortgagee) to secure repayment of a loan or to ensure satisfaction of a debt.

Mortgage broker. A finance professional who seeks to obtain the best rates and terms on behalf of a borrower but is not a party to the transaction. Mortgage brokers can play a valuable role in securing the best possible funding for a borrower's needs.

Mortgage insurance. See *lenders mortgage insurance (LMI)*.

Packages. Packages are products that combine a number of banking facilities, such as a bank account, credit card and loan(s), for one annual fee – plus, they offer a mortgage interest-rate discount which is dependent on the customer's total lending. Packages are particularly advantageous for investors (perhaps with multiple loans) because you don't have to pay an application fee or additional ongoing fees.

Pre-approval. A pre-approval is when a bank has reviewed your loan application and given you indicative approval to borrow a certain amount, at a certain *LVR*, before you've found a property. This not only saves you (and your broker) time and stress, it also puts you in a position of strength compared to other potential purchasers, as you can be reasonably sure your finance will be approved.

Principal and interest (P&I) loans. With a P&I loan, borrowers are required to make regular, predetermined repayments on the principal and interest components of the loan so that the principal is fully repaid within a certain period (usually 30 years). See also *interest-only loans*.

Private lenders. Wealthy private individuals or businesses that have money available to lend out as mortgages. In the past, private lending was typically conducted through solicitors' funds, where the solicitor might have a number of wealthy clients whose money was pooled together and then lent to private clients (acting in much the same way as a mortgage manager).

Registered mortgage debenture (RMD). A fixed and floating charge over an entity's assets.

Security. An asset pledged to guarantee the repayment of a loan in compliance with an agreement. Security gives a lender legal right of access to the pledged asset and the right to take possession and title if the loan is defaulted on (i.e. repayments are not made).

Self-managed superannuation fund (SMSF). A trust established for one to four people in which cash and investments are held for the principal purpose of funding the members' retirement.

Serviceability. The degree to which the servicing of a loan (i.e. the repayments can be made) can be accomplished with given resources and within a specified time frame.

Solicitors' funds. See *private lenders*.

Title (of property). The legal document recording a person's right to ownership of a property. There are various forms of title, with particular characteristics, e.g. Torrens Title, Green Title, Strata, Company share, Community and Old System Title.

Trust deed. The document governing how a trust should be managed, who is to manage it and who will benefit from the profits generated by assets of the trust.

Trustee. An individual or entity which holds and manages assets on trust for the benefit of another/others (the beneficiary(ies)).

INDEX

TrackMySPEND 28
trusts 105, 106–09
—family 182, 199–200
—hybrid 200
—loans to 199
—simple structure 107
—unit 204

UBank 9
underperforming
 properties 173
unit trusts 110

vacancy rates 29, 142
—commercial property 190
valuations 45, 101, 143, 180,
 202–03
—cost of 90, 148
—bank policies 146–47
—for commercial finance
 190–91
—how to maximise 148–49,
 151, 203
—low 94, 147
—types 146

variable-rate loans 68, 197
—basic 54–55
—standard 55
Victoria Teachers Credit
 Union 8
Volt Bank 10

wealth-building 195
Westpac 3, 4, 186
wholesale lending 2, 8
Wizard 4
Woolworths Employees'
 Credit Union 7

Xinja Bank 10

Yardney, Michael 175

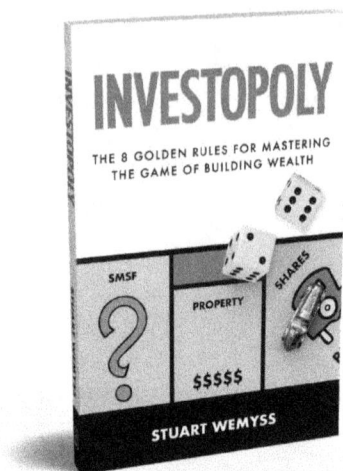

ALSO BY STUART WEMYSS

To win at Monopoly, you need a little luck, but you also need to apply certain rules – like buying as much property as possible, not spending all your cash and negotiating to get a full set of properties as soon as you can.

Building wealth is no different! You can win at the game of building personal wealth by applying Stuart Wemyss' **8 Golden Rules**, tested and refined over two decades.

Stuart possesses the rare skill of being able to make financial planning interesting, and provides easy-to-understand information to help you plan, save and invest for a comfortable lifestyle and financial security.

Visit goodreads.com and books.google.com.au to read glowing reviews of *Investopoly*.

Available at majorstreet.com.au and all good bookstores.

ISBN: 9780648238720 RRP: $29.95

www.ingramcontent.com/pod-product-compliance
Lightning Source LLC
Chambersburg PA
CBHW031925190326
41519CB00007B/418